NEW DIMENSIONS OF PUBLIC RELATION AND PRESS

NEW DIMENSIONS OF PUBLIC RELATION AND PRESS

By

Sanjeev Gulati

2008

CYBER TECH PUBLICATIONS
4264/3, Ansari Road, Daryaganj, New Delhi-110002 (India)
Ph.: 011-23244078. Fax: 011-23280028
E-Mail: cyberpublicationsdelhi@yahoo.com

NEW DIMENSIONS OF PUBLIC RELATION AND PRESS

Sanjeev Gulati

First Edition 2008

Published by :

G.S. Rawat for Cyber Tech Publications
4264/3, Ansari Road, Daryaganj, New Delhi-110002 (India)
Ph.: 011-23244078. Fax: 011-23280028
E-Mail: cyberpublicationsdelhi@yahoo.com

Preface

Public relations is the managing of outside communication of an organization or business to create and maintain a positive image. Public relations involves popularizing successes, downplaying failures, announcing changes, and many other activities. The First World War also helped stimulate the development of public relations as a profession. Modern public relations uses a variety of techniques including opinion polling and focus groups to evaluate public opinion, combined with a variety of high-tech techniques for distributing information on behalf of their clients, including satellite feeds, the Internet, broadcast faxes, and database-driven phone banks to recruit supporters for a client's cause.

Although public relations professionals are stereotypically seen as corporate servants, the reality is that almost any organization that has a stake in how it is portrayed in the public arena employs at least one PR manager. Large organizations may even have dedicated communications departments. Government agencies, trade associations, and other non-profit organizations commonly carry out PR activities.

Public relations should be seen as a management function in any organization. An effective communication, or public relations, plan for an organization is developed to communicate to an audience (whether internal or external publics) in such a way the message coincides with organizational goals and seeks to benefit mutual interests whenever possible.

In this book the author has endeavoured to bring all necessary facts in comprehensible yet in a lucid manner.

Suggestions of the readers are always welcome.

—Author

Contents

1

INTRODUCTION

Public relations (PR) is the managing of outside communication of an organization or business to create and maintain a positive image. Public relations involves popularizing successes, downplaying failures, announcing changes, and many other activities.

DEFINITION

The term Public Relations was first used by the US President Thomas Jefferson during his address to Congress in 1807.

One of the earliest definitions of PR was created by Edward Bernays. According to him, "Public Relations is a management function which tabulates public attitudes, defines the policies, procedures and interest of an organization followed by executing a program of action to earn public understanding and acceptance."

Examples/users of public relations include:

- Corporations using marketing public relations (MPR) to convey information about the products they manufacture or services they provide to potential customers in order to support their direct sales efforts. Typically, they support sales in the short to long term, establishing and burnishing the corporation's branding for a strong, ongoing market.

- Corporations using public relations as a vehicle to reach legislators and other politicians, in seeking favourable tax, regulatory, and other treatment. Moreover, they may use public relations to portray themselves as enlightened employers, in support of human-resources recruiting programs.
- Non-profit organizations, including schools and universities, hospitals, and human and social service agencies: such organizations may make use of public relations in support of awareness programs, fund-raising programs, staff recruiting, and to increase patronage of their services.
- Politicians aiming to attract votes and/or raise money. When such campaigns are successful at the ballot box, this helps in promoting and defending their service in office, with an eye to the next election or, at a career's end, to their legacy.

Today "Public Relations is a set of management, surpervisory, and technical functions that foster an organization's ability to strategically listen to, appreciate, and respond to those persons whose mutually beneficial relationships with the organization are necessary if it is to achieve its missions and values." (Robert L. Heath, Encyclopedia of Public Relations). Essentially it is a management function that focuses on two-way communication and fostering of mutually beneficial relationships between an organization and its publics. There is a school of public relations that holds that it is about relationship management. Phillips, explored this concept in his paper "Towards relationship management: Public relations at the core of organisational development" paper in 2006 which lists a range of academics and practitioners who support this view.

HISTORY

Precursors: Evidence of the practices used in modern day public relations are scattered through history. One notable practitioner was Georgiana Cavendish, Duchess of Devonshire whose efforts on behalf of Charles James Fox in the 18th century included press relations, lobbying and, with her friends, celebrity campaigning. A member of the Spencer family, she shares a family celebrity trait with Diana, Princess of Wales.

A number of American precursors to public relations are, found in publicists who specialized in promoting circuses, theatrical performances, and other public spectacles. In the United States, where public relations has its origins, many early PR practices were developed in support of the expansive power of the railroads. In fact, many scholars believe that the first appearance of the term "public relations" appeared in the 1897 Year Book of Railway Literature.

Later, PR practitioners were-and are still often-recruited from the ranks of journalism. Some reporters, concerned with ethics, criticize former colleagues for using their inside understanding of news media to help clients receive favourable media coverage.

Despite many journalists' discomfort with the field of public relations, well-paid PR positions remain a popular choice for reporters and editors forced into a career change by the instability and often fewer economic opportunities provided by the print and electronic media industry.

THE FIRST "NAMES"

The First World War also helped stimulate the development of public relations as a profession. Many of the first PR professionals, including Ivy Lee, Edward Bernays, John Hill, and Carl Byoir, got their start with the Committee on Public Information (also known as the Creel Commission), which organized publicity on behalf of U.S. objectives during World War I. Some historians regard Ivy Lee as the first real practitioner of public relations, but Edward Bernays is generally regarded today as the profession's founder. In describing the origin of the term Public Relations, Bernays commented, "When I came back to the United States, I decided that if you could use propaganda for war, you could certainly use it for peace. And propaganda got to be a bad word because of the Germans.. using it. So what I did was to try to find some other words, so we found the words Council on Public Relations".

Ivy Lee, who has been credited with developing the modern news release (also called a "press release"), espoused a philosophy consistent with what has sometimes been called the "two-way street" approach to public relations, in which PR consists of helping clients listen as well as communicate messages to their publics. In the words of the Public Relations Society of America (PRSA), "Public relations helps an organization and its publics adapt mutually to each other." In practice, however, Lee often engaged in one-way propagandizing on behalf of clients despised by the public, including Standard Oil founder John D. Rockefeller. Shortly before his death, the US Congress had been investigating his work on behalf of the controversial Nazi German company IG Farben.

In the 1890s when gender role reversals could be caricaturized, the idea of an aggressive woman who also smoked was considered laughable. In 1929, Edward Bernays proved otherwise when he convinced women to smoke in public during an Easter parade in Manhattan as a show of defiance against male domination. The demonstrators were not aware that a tobacco company was behind the publicity stunt.

Bernays was the profession's first theorist. A nephew of Sigmund Freud, Bernays drew many of his ideas from Freud's theories about the irrational, unconscious motives that shape human behaviour. Bernays authored several books, including Crystallizing Public Opinion (1923), Propaganda (1928), and The Engineering of Consent (1947). Bernays saw public relations as an "applied social science" that uses insights from psychology, sociology, and other disciplines to scientifically manage and manipulate the thinking and behaviour of an irrational and "herdlike" public. "The conscious and intelligent manipulation of the organized habits and opinions of the masses is an important element in democratic society," he wrote in Propaganda. "Those who manipulate this unseen mechanism of society constitute an invisible government which is the true ruling power of our country."

One of Bernays' early clients was the tobacco industry. In 1929, he orchestrated a legendary publicity stunt aimed at persuading women to take up cigarette smoking, an act that at the time was exclusively equated with men. It was considered unfeminine and inappropriate for women to smoke, besides the occasional prostitute, virtually no women participated in the act publicly.

Bernays initially consulted psychoanalyst A. A. Brill for advice, Brill told him: "Some women regard cigarettes as symbols of freedom... Smoking is a sublimation of oral eroticism; holding a cigarette in the mouth excites the oral zone. It is perfectly normal for women to want to smoke cigarettes. Further the first women who smoked probably had an excess of male components and adopted the habit as a masculine act. But today the emancipation of women has suppressed many feminine desires. More women now do the same work as men do.... Cigarettes, which are equated with men, become torches of freedom."

Upon hearing this analysis, Bernays dubbed his PR campaign the: "Torches of Liberty Contingent".

It was in this spirit that Bernays arranged for New York City débutantes to march in that year's Easter Day Parade, defiantly smoking cigarettes as a statement of rebellion against the norms of a male-dominated society. Publicity photos of these beautiful fashion models smoking "Torches of Liberty" were sent to various media outlets and appeared worldwide. As a result, the taboo was dissolved and many women were led to associate the act of smoking with female liberation. Some women went so far as to demand membership in all-male smoking clubs, a highly controversial act at the time.

For his work, Bernays was paid a tidy sum by George Washington Hill, president of the American Tobacco Company.

PROFESSIONAL STANDARDS

In 1950 PRSA enacts the first "Professional Standards for the Practice of Public Relations," a forerunner to the current Code of Ethics, last revised in 2000 to include six core values and six code provisions. The six core values are "Advocacy, Honesty, Expertise, Independence, Loyalty, and Fairness." The six code provisions consulted with are "Free Flow of Information, Competition, Disclosure of Information, Safeguarding Confidences, Conflicts of Interest, and Enhancing the Profession."

In 1982 effective Public Relations helped save the Johnson & Johnson Corporation, after the highly publicized Tylenol poisoning crisis.

The Industry Today

Modern public relations uses a variety of techniques including opinion polling and focus groups to evaluate public opinion, combined with a variety of high-tech techniques for distributing information on behalf of their clients, including satellite feeds, the Internet, broadcast faxes, and database-driven phone banks to recruit supporters for a client's cause. According to the PRSA,

> *"Examples of the knowledge that may be required in the professional practice of public relations include communication arts, psychology, social psychology, sociology, political science, economics, and the*

principles of management and ethics. Technical knowledge and skills are required for opinion research, public issues analysis, media relations, direct mail, institutional advertising, publications, film/video productions, special events, speeches, and presentations."

Although public relations professionals are stereotypically seen as corporate servants, the reality is that almost any organization that has a stake in how it is portrayed in the public arena employs at least one PR manager. Large organizations may even have dedicated communications departments. Government agencies, trade associations, and other non-profit organizations commonly carry out PR activities.

Public relations should be seen as a management function in any organization. An effective communication, or public relations, plan for an organization is developed to communicate to an audience (whether internal or external publics) in such a way the message coincides with organizational goals and seeks to benefit mutual interests whenever possible.

As industry consolidation becomes more prevalent, many organizations and individuals are choosing to retain "boutique" firms as opposed to so-called "global" communications firms. These smaller firms typically specialize in only a couple of practice areas and thus, often have a greater understanding of their client's business. And because they deal with certain journalists with greater frequency, speciality firms often have stronger media contacts in the areas that matter most to their clients. Added benefits of smaller, specialty firms include more personal attention and accountability and as well, cost savings. This is not to say that smaller is always better, but there is a growing consensus that specialty firms offer more than once considered.

SPECIALITIES OF PUBLIC RELATIONS

A number of specialities exist within the field of public relations, including:

Crisis Management

Crisis management involves identifying a crisis, planning a response to the crisis and confronting and resolving the crisis. Crisis management can be applied in almost any field of endeavour, but it is most commonly used in international relations, political science, business and management. For more about crisis management in international relations, see International crisis.

Many school districts have developed crisis response guides, which identify potential situations such as fires and other disasters, bomb threats, confronting unwelcome visitors, violence (and threats thereof) and the death of a student.

In general terms, the theory of crisis management can be divided into crisis bargaining and negotiation, crisis decision making, and crisis dynamics. In a crisis, always sit down and think hard about your decision, and for as long as needed (or allowed) about ways in which you can resolve it.

It has to be you that applies even if somebody else has to carry the burden of action-how you brief, direct and control the other or other will vital to the outcome.

In Business

In business there are three main types of crisis:

- Financial crisis-short term liquidity or cash flow problems; and long term bankruptcy problems
- Public relations crisis-More commonly called "crisis communications," negative publicity that could adversely affect the success of the company
- Strategic crisis-changes in the business environment that call the viability of the company into question-

for example the introduction of the automobile was a strategic crisis for buggy-whip manufacturers

Certain preliminary measures need to be taken to prevent a crisis. Companies should always plan ahead and project likely outcomes. They should avoid decisions that have the potential to turn into a crisis. They should know their "worst case scenarios" and have a contingency plan for it.

If prevention has not been successful, then the following six steps should be undertaken immediately:

- Do an objective assessment of the cause(s) of the crisis.
- Determine whether the cause(s) will have a long term effect or whether it will be a short term phenomena.
- Project the most likely course of events.
- Focus all the most capable people (including yourself) on activities that will mitigate or eliminate the problem.
- Look for opportunities-there could be a "silver lining".
- Immediately act to guard cash flow.

If it is a cashflow crisis do not wait for further evidence before acting. Immediately take actions to maintain or increase cash flow. These could include:

- accelerating accounts receivable payments even if this requires the granting of discounts
- decelerating accounts payable payments even if this means losing discounts
- increasing short term sales
- maintaining or increasing profit margins on sales if possible
- reducing expenses:
    * eliminating non-essential expenses
    * selling non-mission critical assets

  * reducing payroll
  * outsourcing non-mission critical operations
- renegotiating loans and other debts wherever possible-obtaining interest-only loans or extended payment terms

If it is a public relations crisis, act immediately to prevent or counter the spread of the negative information. Containment may require intense media activities. Use every media available to you to provide a counter argument or question the credibility of the original negative publicity.

Reputation Management

Reputation management is the process of tracking an entity's actions and other entities' opinions about those actions; reporting on those actions and opinions; and reacting to that report creating a feedback loop. All entities involved are generally people, but that need not always be the case. Other examples of entities include animals, businesses, or even locations or materials. The tracking and reporting may range from word-of-mouth to statistical analysis of thousands data points.

Reputation management has come into wide use with the advent of widespread computing. Reputation management systems use various predefined criteria for processing complex data to report reputation. However, these systems only facilitate and automate some aspects the process of determing trustworthiness. This process is central to all kinds of human interaction, including interpersonal relationships, international diplomacy, stock markets, and sports.

Real-world Communities

Small Town

The classic example of reputation management is the small town. Population is small and interactions between members frequent; most interactions are face-to-face and positively identified--that is, there is no question who said or did what. Reputation accrues not only throughout one's lifetime, but is passed down to one's offspring; one's individual reputation depends both on one's own actions and one's inherited reputation.

There are generally few formal mechanisms to manage this implicit reputation. The town diner and barber shop serve as forums for exchange of gossip, in which community members' reputations are discussed, often in frank terms. Outstanding members may receive small, symbolic awards or titles, but these are mere confirmations of general knowledge.

There is exceedingly little deviation from community norms in a small town. This may be seen as either good or bad; there is little crime, but also little room for dissent or change. The small-town model scales poorly; it depends on each member having enough experience of a large number of other members, and this is only possible up to a point.

Big City

The large metropolitan area is at the other end of the spectrum from the small rural town. Community members come and go daily, and most members are only personally acquainted with a small fraction of the whole. Implicit reputation management continues to work within subcommunities, but for the city as a whole, it cannot.

Big cities have developed a large array of formal reputation management methods. Some apply only to subcommunities, such as, say, an association of local dentists. There are four methods (among others) which apply quite generally to the entire population: elections, appointments, the criminal justice system, and racial or ethnic prejudice.

- The city is governed in part by elected officials--persons who are given special powers by popular vote at regular intervals. Campaigns are often well-financed efforts to force a positive image of a candidate's reputation upon the electorate; television is often decisive. Elected officials are primarily concerned with preserving this good reputation, which concern dictates their every public action. Failure to preserve a good reputation, not to mention failure to avoid a bad one, is often cause for removal from office, sometimes prematurely. Candidates and officials frequently concentrate on damaging the reputations of their opponents.

- Appointed officials are not elected; they are granted special powers, usually by elected officials, without public deliberation. Persons wishing to be appointed to office also campaign to increase their perceived reputation, but the audience is much smaller. Effective actions and demonstrated merit are often important factors in gaining a positive reputation, but the definition of this merit is made by the elected, appointing officials, who tend to evaluate merit as it applies to them, personally. Thus persons who work hard to increase an elected official's reputation increase their own, at least in their patron's eyes. Some appointees have no other qualification beyond the fact that they may be depended on at all times to support their patrons.
- The stresses of big city life lead to much crime, which demands punishment, on several grounds. The severity of this punishment and of the efforts of the system to inflict it upon a community member depends in no small part on that individual's prior experiences within the system. Elaborate records are kept of every infraction, even of the suspicion of infractions, and these records are consulted before any decision is made, no matter how trivial. Great effort is expended to positively identify members--driver's licenses and fingerprints, for example--and any use of an alias is carefully recorded. Some small punishments are meted

out informally, but most punishments, especially severe ones, are given only after a long, detailed, and formal process: a trial, which must result in a conviction, or finding of guilt, before a punishment is ordered.

Although it is sometimes said that serving one's punishment is sufficient penalty for the commission of a crime, in truth the damage to one's reputation may be the greater penalty--damage both within the system itself and within other systems of urban reputation management, such as that of elections to office. Between the explicit punishment and the damage to one's reputation, the total effect of a conviction in the criminal justice system so damages a person's ability to lead a normal life that the process, at least ostensibly, is meticulous in determining guilt or lack thereof. In case of "reasonable" doubt, a suspected malefactor is freed--though the mere fact of the trial is recorded, and affects his future reputation.

- The ordinary citizen, meeting a stranger, another citizen unknown to the first, is rarely concerned that the second may be an official, elected or otherwise; even so, he may be aware of the relative failure of reputation management in this regard. He does not have easy access to the database of the criminal justice system, and portions are not publicly available at all. Lacking other means, he often turns to the mock-system of racial or ethnic prejudice. This attempts to extend the small-town model to large communities by grouping individuals who look alike, dress alike, or talk alike. One reputation serves for all. Each individual is free to compose his personal measure of a group's reputation, and actions of strangers raise or lower that reputation for all group members.

The high incidence of crime, the proverbial incompetence of officials, and constant wars between rival, self-identified groups speaks poorly of all systems of urban reputation management. Together, they do not function as well as that of the small town, with no formal system at all.

ISSUE MANAGEMENT

In public relations, issue management is the process used to align organizational activities and stakeholder expectations. Issue managers work in government affairs, legal affairs, public affairs and regulatory compliance.

In business, Issue Management refers to the discipline and process of managing business issues and usually implies using technology to electronically automate the process. Electronic issue management has gathered steam as a business and technology movement in recent years as mid-sized and large businesses have realized the advantage of implementing systems to manage, document, and track work.

Early examples of issue management systems appeared in the late 1980s with customer ticketing systems. Businesses that implemented these systems were often addressing customer complaints and needed a method to document, track, and manage to complaints to successful resolution. These systems evolved and with the widespread introduction of Information Technology departments that further pushed issue management systems with advent of 'help desk' systems.

Today, issue management systems are commonly used by product development companies to manage requests, changes to products, reported defects, etc.

A typical issue workflow might look like this with regard to issue state: [issue submitted]→ [open]→ [in evaluation]→ [in work]→ [in test]→ [closed] Where the [in test] and [in work] phases often loop.

A typical issue management electronic workflow might look like this with regard to roles:

1. An issue is submitted by a customer, salesperson, engineer, or test engineer, often via a web browser.

2. The issue management system logs the issue and relocates the issue to a predefined representative's inbox.
3. The representative evaluates the issue and assigns it to an appropriate employee.
4. Work is done on the issue, documented in the system, and closed.
5. In most processes, the originator is notified that the issue has been resolved.

Any issue management process in which there are well defined inputs and outputs can be automated electronically.

There are both private and open source solutions available to companies interested in implementing issue management.

Unfortunately, open source issue management systems are not making good progress catching up with the solutions available privately. At the time of this writing they have not incorporated important system features related to project integration. Specifically, open source solutions haven't delivered features that contextualize issues as a part of an overall project, incorporate dependent and transitional fields, and support multiple workflows within a single interface.

INVESTOR RELATIONS

Investor relations is a set of activities which relate to the ways in which a company discloses information required for regulatory compliance and good investment judgment to bond and/or shareholders and the wider financial markets. Investor relations is considered a specialty of public relations by the U.S. Department of Labour.

Most public quoted companies now have dedicated IR officers or managers who looks after the company's investor relations activities and deal with investors wishing to know more about the company. Functions of investor relations personnel often include collection of information on competitors and dissemination of information via press conferences, one-on-one briefings, investor relations sections of company websites, and company annual reports. The investor relations function also often includes the transmission of information relating to intangible values such as the company's policy to corporate governance and its wider corporate social responsibility.

The investor relations function must be aware of current and up-coming issues which the organization may face, and which may have an impact on the organization. In particular, it must be able to assess the likely impact or reaction of any announcements (or any research reports issued by Financial analysts) to be made on the share price of a company. It will have top-level access to the Chief Executive Officer and Chairman or President of the corporation to ensure that the image of the corporation is maintained in a coherent fashion.

Due to the potential impact of legal liability claims awarded by courts, and the consequential impact on the company's share price, IR often has a role in crisis management of, for example, product liability issues and industrial disasters.

The professional body for Investor Relations in the U.S. is the National Investor Relations Institute known as NIRI. In the United Kingdom, the recognised industry body is the Investor Relations Society, while in Australia the professional body is the Australian Investor Relations Association and in Canada the professional association is called CIRI (Canadian Investor Relations Institute).

The Sarbanes-Oxley Act

The Sarbanes-Oxley Act of 2002 increased the duties and roles of investor relations professionals. The act established new requirements for corporate governance, reporting, and disclosure and it added significant new criminal and civil penalties for non-compliance. Notable provisions of the act which apply to investor relations include enhanced financial disclosures and accuracy of financial reports, real-time disclosures, off-balance sheet transaction disclosures, pro forma financial disclosures, management assessment of internal controls, and corporate responsibility for financial reports.

Industrial Relations

The field of industrial relations looks at the relationship between management and workers, particularly groups of workers represented by a union.

Labour relations is an important factor in analyzing "varieties of capitalism", such as neocorporatism (or corporatism), social democracy, and neoliberalism (or liberalism).

Labour relations can take place on many levels, such as the "shop-floor", the regional level, and the national level. The distribution of power amongst these levels can greatly shape the way an economy functions.

Another key question when considering systems of labour relations is their ability to adapt to change. This change can be technological (e.g., "What do we do when an industry employing half the population becomes obsolete?"), economic (e.g., "How do we respond to globalization?"), or political (e.g., "How dependent is the system on a certain party or coalition holding power?").

Governments set the framework for labour relations through legislation and regulation. Usually, employment law would cover issues such as minimum wages and wrongful dismissal.

Industrial relations is the equivalent term in Australia, though in recent years the term workplace relations has also become common. This has become a prominent issue of late as the Liberal Government introduced Work Choices to gear the Australian economy for the future.

Perspective Theories

When studying the theories of industrial relations, there are three major perspectives that contrast in their approach to the nature of workplace relations. The three views are generally described as the unitary, pluralist and Marxist perspectives. The Marxist perspective is sometimes referred to as the Conflict Model. Each offers a particular perception of workplace relations and will therefore interpret such events as workplace conflict, the role of trade unions and job regulation very differently.

Unitary Perspective

In unitarism, the organisation is perceived as an integrated and harmonious whole with the ideal of "one happy family", where management and other members of the staff all share a common purpose, emphasising mutual cooperation. Furthermore, unitarism has a paternalistic approach where it demands loyalty of all employees, being predominantly managerial in its emphasis and application.

Consequently, trade unions are deemed as unnecessary since the loyalty between trade unions and organisations are considered mutually exclusive, where there can't be two sides of industry. Conflict is perceived as disruptive and the pathological result of agitators, interpersonal friction and communication breakdown.

Pluralistic Perspective

In pluralism the organisation is perceived as being made up of powerful and divergent sub-groups, each with its own legitimate loyalties and with their own set of objectives and leaders. In particular, the two predominant sub-groups of in the pluralistic perspective are the management and trade unions.

Consequently, the role of management would lean less towards enforcing and controlling and more toward persuasion and co-ordination. Trade unions are deemed as legitimate representatives of employees, conflict is dealt by collective bargaining and is viewed not necessarily as a bad thing and if managed could in fact be channelled towards evolution and positive change.

Marxist Perspective

This view of industrial relations looks the nature of the capitalist society, where there is a fundamental division of interest between capital and labour, and sees workplace relations against this background. This perspective sees inequalities of power and economic wealth as having their roots in the nature of the capitalist economic system. Conflict is therefore seen as inevitable and trade unions are a natural response of workers to their exploitation by capital. Whilst there may be periods of acquiescence, the Marxist view would be that institutions of joint regulation would enhance rather limit managements position as they presume the continuation of capitalism rather than challenge it.

2

ASTROTURFING

MEANING AND DEFINITION

Astroturfing is a term for formal public relations campaigns in politics and advertising that seek to create the impression of being spontaneous, grassroots behaviour. Hence the reference to Astro Turf (artificial grass) is a metaphor to indicate fake grassroots support.

The goal of such a campaign is to disguise the agenda of a client as an independent public reaction to some political entity-a politician, political group, product, service or event. Astroturfers attempt to orchestrate the actions of apparently diverse and geographically distributed individuals, by both overt ("outreach," "awareness," etc.) and covert (disinformation) means. Astroturfing may be undertaken by anything from an individual pushing their own personal agenda through to highly organized professional groups with financial backing from large corporations, non-profits, or activist organizations.

Origin of the Term

The term, said to have been used first in this context by former U.S. Senator Lloyd Bentsen, is wordplay based on "grassroots democracy" efforts, which are truly spontaneous undertakings largely sustained by private persons (not politicians, governments, corporations, or public relations firms). "Astro Turf" refers to the bright green artificial grass used in some sports stadiums, so "astroturfing" refers to artificial grassroots efforts.

TECHNIQUES

A form of propaganda, astroturfing attempts to affect selectively the emotions of the public, whether trying to win a campaign, be the top music record seller, be the top book seller, or gain political support.

Astroturfing techniques usually consist of a few people discreetly posing as mass numbers of activists advocating a specific cause.

It has become easier to structure an astroturfing campaign in the electronic era because the cost and effort to send an e-mail (especially a pre-written, sign-your-name-at-the-bottom e-mail) is so low. Companies may use a boiler room full of telephones and computers where hired activists locate people and groups that create enthusiasm for the specified cause. Also, the use of psychographics allows hired supporters to persuade their targeted audience.

Examples

Early Examples

At the turn of the 20th century, it was common to have newspapers in major American cities sponsored by local political parties. Some were open about this practice, but many of these relationships were hidden. Other examples include political "clubs" which front for voter fraud and intimidation, letter-writing campaigns organized by local ward bosses, and some union-organized political activities.

In one case, documented in the book All the President's Men, the Committee to Re-Elect the President orchestrated several campaigns of "public support" for decisions made by President Nixon in the period preceding the 1972 election, including telegrams to the White House and an apparently independent advertisement placed in The New York Times.

King Léopold II of Belgium used extensive astro Turf lobbying in the US and Europe to facilitate his economic exploitation of the Congo. (Adam Hochschild, 1999)

Another case is that of Bolivian dictator General Luis Garcia Meza Tejada, who at the end of his promised one-year rule staged a televised rally and declared "Bueno, me quedo," or in English: "All right, I'll stay."

Manipulation of public opinion was also used in the Soviet Union. Political decisions were often preceded by massive campaigns of orchestrated 'letters from workers' which were quoted and published in newspapers and radio. In Stalin's era, massive "public demonstrations" were organized against "the enemies of the people"; those attending were often forced or intimidated into doing so.

Examples from the 1990s

In 1991 a memo from PR firm van Kloberg & Associates to Zairian ambassador Tatanene Tanata referring to the "Zaire Program 1991" was leaked. The memo outlines steps the firm was taking to improve the image of Mobutu Sese Seko's regime, including placing dozens of letters to the editor, op-ed pieces, and articles in the American press praising the Zairian government.

In 1998, Paul Reitsma, former member of the Legislative Assembly of British Columbia, was accused of writing letters to newspapers under assumed names praising himself and attacking his political opponents. A Parksville newspaper had asked a former RCMP handwriting expert to compare a sample of Reitsma's handwriting to that of letters to the editor submitted by a "Warren Betanko", and then ran a story entitled "MLA Reitsma is a liar and we can prove it". For this, Reitsma was expelled from the caucus of the British Columbia Liberal Party and then compelled to resign his seat after it became obvious that an effort to recall him would succeed.

Recent Examples

- In 2001, the Los Angeles Times accused Microsoft of astroturfing when hundreds of similar letters were sent to newspapers voicing disagreement with the United States Department of Justice and its antitrust suit against Microsoft. The letters, prepared by Americans for Technology Leadership, had in some cases been mailed from deceased citizens or nonexistent addresses. Similar allegations were leveled against the "Freedom to Innovate Network", originally portrayed as an independent grassroots organization but web-hosted by Microsoft.
- In July 2004, RealNetworks tried to press Apple Inc. to open up their FairPlay DRM for the iPod with the Harmony plug-in. The work-around allows users to purchase songs from RealNetworks' Rhapsody and then convert it for use for the iPod. They also setup an internet petition "Hey Apple! Don't break my iPod," and slashed the prices of its songs to below that of iTunes. It backfired, as many posters reacted negatively and accused RealNetworks of astroturfing.
- In March 2006, a supposed environmental group called the Save Our Species Alliance was exposed as a front group that was created by a timber lobbyist to weaken the Endangered Species Act. The campaign director for this group is Tim Wigley, the Executive Director of Pac/West Communications. Wigley was also the campaign director for Project Protect, another front group that spent $2.9 million to help pass President Bush's Healthy Forests legislation which has been criticized for its pro-industry bias. The Save Our Species Alliance web site portrays itself as a grassroots organization against the Endangered Species Act (the word "grassroots" is mentioned no less than five times on their "Take Action Now" page), but is criticized by environmentalists for being a front group for wealthy

cattle and timber interests which consider Federal environmental legislation an impediment to profit.

- In March 2006 video game manufacturers faced over seventy anti-games bills across the country. Embattled, they established the Video Game Voters Network, "a new grassroots political network for gamers" which publicly portrayed itself as a populist effort to lobby State and Federal legislators against supporting violent video game-related legislation. In April 2007 in an interview on video game news website, GameDaily, consumer advocate and founder of the Entertainment Consumers Association (ECA), Hal Halpin, stated that "The Videogame Voters Network is very needed and wanted by the industry, but it's supported by the industry, so it's called "astroturfing" where our organization is grassroots and the difference in the two pieces of terminology is significant when it comes to legislators because they'll look at an astro Turf organization as one that's backed by the industry; funded by them, run by them, organized by them." The following day ESA (Entertainment Software Association) spokesperson Caroyln Rauch responded in a written statement, "...calling the VGVN 'astroturf' is not only counterproductive and just not correct, but it also demeans the passion and energy of its members."
- Since 2006, an organisation calling itself the Palm Oil Truth Foundation and claiming to be 'an international network of social conscience and cooperation among peoples in industry, government, academia and the ordinary global consuming public' has been campaigning to promote the use of palm oil in food, rubbishing negative health claims against the oil and pouring scorn on environmental concerns about the impact of the industry's expansion. Oil Palm is an extremely lucrative tropical crop which has been

accused by many NGOs as being responsible for the rapid destruction of rainforests and orang-utan habitat in Malaysia and Indonesia. The Foundation claims no industry links but is connected to the Malaysian Oil Palm Council (MPOC) through their website. The Foundation's operations are curiously coincidental with a large PR contract tendered by the Malaysian Palm Oil Council to counter the negative image of the industry in Europe.

- In May 2006, SanDisk launched a site called iDon't, appearing to be a blog started by individuals opposed to Apple's domination of the portable music player market. It was actually an advertisement mechanism for their own device, the Sansa e200.
- In August 2006, a science journalist for the Wall Street Journal revealed that a YouTube video-"Al Gore's Penguin Army"-which was claimed to be an amateur work in fact came from the computers of DCI Group, a Washington, D.C.-based PR firm whose acknowledged leaders all have ties to the Republican Party and whose client list includes ExxonMobil and General Motors. (See Al Gore's Penguin Army video controversy.) This hoax was discovered when journalist Antonio Ragalado noticed that the YouTube video was the first sponsored listing when he performed a Google search for Al Gore. The fact that someone was actually paying to have the alleged amateur film promoted was in itself suspicious.
- Since the spring of 2006, American Airlines has received frequent accusations of astroturfing due to its acknowledged support (including some financial backing) of Stop and Think, a Dallas-based organization that has advocated the retention of the federal Wright Amendment ban on most long haul commercial passenger airline service at Dallas Love Field. Many opponents of the Wright Amendment

believe that American, the dominant passenger airline at nearby Dallas/Fort Worth International Airport, has an overly cozy relationship with the management of DFW Airport and/or uses highly aggressive competitive tactics against other airlines that serve DFW, and that for airline competition in North Texas to increase substantively, the federal government must repeal the Wright Amendment and let Love Field be an alternative to DFW for airlines flying long haul routes to and from North Texas. Therefore, these critics think that the Wright Amendment unduly limits the competition that American faces in the North Texas commercial aviation market and that American is using Stop and Think to try to manipulate the public into backing the law--and, by extension, the airline's commercial interests--under a pretense of broad-based community support.

- In July 2006, an article by Vladimir Socor, a veteran analyst of east European affairs for the Jamestown Foundation, claimed that a report on Transnistria issued by the International Council for Democratic Institutions and State Sovereignty, "State Sovereignty of Pridnestrovie (PMR) under international law", was a Russian-sponsored attempt at disinformation. A spokesperson for the organization, Megan Stephenson, has denied these charges. Shortly afterwards The Economist published two articles highlighting the ICDISS's lack of a physical presence and its disinclination to provide independent verification of its activities and previous existence. The Economist also reported that prominent academics cited as sources in the ICDISS report on Transdniestria disclaimed any connection with the organization.
- In December 2006, the "All I want for Xmas is a PSP" marketing campaign by Zipatoni and Sony sparked outrage from the gaming community when it was

discovered that the fake blog was in fact assembled by a marketing team.

- Wake Up Wal-Mart is an organization run by the United Food and Commercial Workers International Union, which seeks to pressure Wal-Mart to yield to the Union's demands. The group's website pages are clearly marked as copyrighted by the UFCW Union, but public statements emphasize instead its "grassroots" nature.
- Wal-Mart Watch is an organization that is mainly funded by Five Stones, a 501(c)(3) organization that received $2,775,000 in 2005 from the SEIU. On their web site, Wal-Mart Watch discloses their association with Five Stones and notes that Andy Stern, the President of the United Food and Commercial Workers International Union, is a member of its board of directors. The SEIU reportedly gave Five Stones $1 million in 2004 to start Wal-Mart Watch.

METHODS, TOOLS, AND TACTICS

Public relations and publicity are not synonyms. Publicity is the spreading of information to gain public awareness in a product, service, candidate, etc. It is just one technique of public relations as listed here.

Audience Targeting

A fundamental technique used in public relations is to identify the target audience, and to tailor every message to appeal to that audience. It can be a general, nationwide or worldwide audience, but it is more often a segment of a population. Marketers often refer to economy-driven "demographics," such as "white males 18-49," but in public relations an audience is more fluid, being whoever someone wants to reach. For example, recent political audiences include "soccer moms" and "NASCAR dads."

In addition to audiences, there are usually stakeholders, literally people who have a "stake" in a given issue. All audiences are stakeholders (or presumptive stakeholders), but not all stakeholders are audiences. For example, a charity commissions a PR agency to create an advertising campaign to raise money to find a cure for a disease. The charity and the people with the disease are stakeholders, but the audience is anyone who is likely to donate money.

Sometimes the interests of differing audiences and stakeholders common to a PR effort necessitate the creation of several distinct but still complementary messages. This is not always easy to do, and sometimes-especially in politics-a spokesperson or client says something to one audience that angers another audience or group of stakeholders.

Publicity

Publicity is the deliberate attempt to manage the public's perception of a subject. The subjects of publicity include people (for example, politicians and performing artists), goods and services, organizations of all kinds, and works of art or entertainment. From a marketing perspective, publicity is one component of promotion. The other elements of the promotional mix are advertising, sales promotion, and personal selling. Promotion is one component of marketing.

Between the client and selected target audiences, publicity is the management of product-or brand-related communications between the firm and the general public. It is primarily an informative activity (as opposed to a persuasive one), but its ultimate goal is to promote the client's products, services, or brands. A publicity plan is a planned program aimed at obtaining favourable media coverage for an organization's products-or for the organization itself, to enhance its reputation and relationships with stakeholders.

A basic tool of the publicist is the press release, but other techniques include telephone press conferences, in-studio media tours, multi-component video news releases (VNR's), newswire stories, and internet releases. For these releases to be used by the media, they must be of interest to the public (or at least to the market segment that the media outlet is targeted to). The releases are often customized to match the media vehicle that they are being sent to. Getting noticed by the press is all about saying the right thing at the right time. A publicist is continuously asking what about you or your company will pique the reader's curiosity and make a good story? The most successful publicity releases are related to topics of current interest. These are referred to as news pegs. An example is if three people die of water poisoning, an alert publicist would release stories about the technology embodied in a water purification product.

But the publicist cannot wait around for the news to present opportunities. They must also try to create their own news. Examples of this include:

- Contests
- Art exhibitions
- Event sponsorship
- Arrange a speech or talk
- Make an analysis or prediction
- Conduct a poll or survey
- Issue a report
- Take a stand on a controversial subject
- Arrange for a testimonial
- Announce an appointment
- Celebrate an anniversary
- Invent then present an award
- Stage a debate
- Organize a tour of your business or projects
- Issue a commendation

The advantages of publicity are low cost, and credibility (particularly if the publicity is aired in between news stories like on evening TV news casts). New technologies such as weblogs, web cameras, web affiliates, and convergence (phone-camera posting of pictures and videos to websites) are changing the cost-structure. The disadvantages are lack of control over how your releases will be used, and frustration over the low percentage of releases that are taken up by the media.

Publicity draws on several key themes including birth, love, and death. These are of particular interest because they are themes in human lives which feature heavily throughout life. In television serials several couples have emerged during crucial ratings and important publicity times, as a way to make constant headlines. Also known as a publicity stunt, the pairings may or may not be truthful.

Publicists

A publicist is a person whose job is to generate and manage publicity for a product, public figure, especially a celebrity, or for a work such as a book or movie. Publicists usually work at large companies handling multiple clients.

Effectiveness of Publicity

The theory any press is good press has been coined to describe situations where bad behaviour by people involved with an organization or brand has actually resulted in positive results, due to the fame and press coverage accrued by such events.

A good example would be Paris Hilton's many antics, from lurid sex tapes to clumsy behaviour on TV shows actually increasing business at the family's chain of Hilton Hotels.

Another example would be the Australian Tourism Board's "So where the Bloody Hell are you?" Advertising Campaign that was initially banned in the UK, but the amount of publicity this generated resulted in the official website for the campaign being swamped with requests to see the banned ad.

The popular sitcom, Married... with Children, achieved skyrocketing ratings after moralist Terry Rakolta attempted to have it removed from the air. It's reported that the former producers send her a fruit basket every Christmas as a gesture of gratitude....

NEWS RELEASE

A news release, press release or press statement is a written or recorded communication directed at members of the news media for the purpose of announcing something claimed as having news value. Typically, it is mailed, faxed, or e-mailed to assignment editors at newspapers, magazines, radio stations, television stations, and/or television networks. Commercial press-release distribution services are also used to distribute news releases. Sometimes news releases are sent for the purpose of announcing news conferences.

A news release is different from a news article. A news article is a compilation of facts developed by journalists published in the news media, whereas a news release is designed to be sent to journalists in order to encourage them to develop articles on the subject. A news release is generally biased towards the objectives of the author.

The use of news releases is common in the field of public relations, the aim of which is to attract favourable media attention to the PR firm's client, and publicity, the aim of which is to attract favourable media attention for products marketed by the client.

Origins

One anecdote on an origin of modern press releases is about an incident in 1906 involving Ivy Lee, who is often referred to as the first real public relations practitioner. At that time, Lee's agency was working with the Pennsylvania Railroad, which had just fallen victim to a tragic accident. Ivy Lee convinced the company to issue the first press release to journalists, before other versions of the story, or suppositions, could be spread among them and reported. He used a press release, in addition to inviting journalists and photographers to the scene and providing their transportation there, as a means of fostering open communication with the media.

Elements

While there are several types of press releases (such as general news releases, event releases, product press releases, and more recently social media press releases), press releases very often have several traits of their structure in common. This helps journalists separate press releases from other PR communication methods, such as pitch letters or media advisories. Some of these common structural elements include:

- Headline-used to grab the attention of journalists and briefly summarize the news.
- Dateline-contains the release date and usually the originating city of the press release.
- Introduction-first paragraph in a press release, that generally gives basic answers to the questions of who, what, when, where and why.
- Body-further explanation, statistics, background, or other details relevant to the news.
- Boilerplate-generally a short "about" section, providing independent background on the issuing company, organization, or individual.
- Close-in North America, traditionally the symbol "-30-" appears after the boilerplate or body and before the media contact information, indicating to media that the release is ending. A more modern equivalent

has been the "###" symbol. In other countries, other means of indicating the end of the release may be used, such as the text "ends".

- Media Contact Information-name, phone number, email address, mailing address, or other contact information for the PR or other media relations contact person.

Video News Releases

Some public relations firms send out video news releases (VNRs) which are pre-taped video programs that can be aired intact by TV stations. Often, the VNRs are aired without the stations' identifying or attributing them as such.

TV news viewers can often detect the use of VNRs within television newscasts; for example, many movie-star "interviews" are actually VNRs, taped on a set which is located at the movie studio and decorated with the movie's logo. Another frequent example of VNRs masquerading as news footage is videotapes of particular medical "breakthroughs," that are really produced and distributed by pharmaceutical companies for the purpose of selling new medicines. Video News Releases can be in the form of full blown productions costing tens of thousands or even hundreds of thousands. They can also be in the TV news format, or even produced for the web.

Recently, many broadcast news outlets have discouraged the use of VNRs. Many stations, citing an already poor public perception, want to increase their credibility. Public relations companies are having a tougher time getting their pre-edited video aired.

VNRs can be turned into podcasts then posted onto newswires. Further to this, a story can be kept running longer by engaging "community websites", which are monitored and commented on by many journalists and features writers.

Criticism

News releases have been a large source of criticism against various types of journalists, who sometimes rely on them heavily. Many articles in the business press, particularly, are little more than recycled press releases. Some people criticize writers for creating articles in this way, contending that it constitutes free advertising for the company on whose behalf the news release was issued, especially if it is not contrasted with criticism of that company or product in the same article. On the other hand, few dispute that news releases remain a valuable way for media to be made aware of new products and services, and recent and upcoming events of interest.

Embargoed News Release

Sometimes a news release is embargoed--that is, news organizations are requested not to report the story until a specified time. For example, news organizations usually receive a copy of presidential speeches several hours in advance. In such cases, the news organizations generally do not break the embargo. If they do, the agency that sent the release may blacklist them. A blacklisted news organization will not receive any more embargoed releases, or possibly any releases at all.

However, it is very hard to enforce embargoes on journalists, as there is constant pressure by editors to be first to a story. It is unlikely that a PR agency will blacklist a form of media, as other clients may want to be featured in this publication. This problem is sometimes overcome by controlling the timing of a release via email rather than relying on the journalist to do so.

Press release format The typical press release announces that the statement is "FOR IMMEDIATE RELEASE" across the top (some may instead be embargoed until a certain date), and lists the issuing organization's media contacts directly below. The media contacts are the people that the release's issuer wants to make available to the media; for example, a press release about new scientific study will typically list the study's lead scientist as its media contact. The bottom of each release is usually marked with ### or-30-to signify the end of the text.

Five "W"s and an "H" There are 6 vital facts to convey in the first paragraph of a release to ensure that it doesn't end up in the bin.

- Who
- What
- When
- Where
- Why
- How

A press release is a written statement distributed to the media. It is a fundamental tool of public relations. Press releases are usually communicated by a newswire service to various news media and journalists may use them as they see fit. Very often the information in a press release finds its way verbatim, or minimally altered, to print and broadcast reports. If a media outlet reports that "John Smith said in a statement today that...", the "statement" usually originated in a press release, or a direct quote from an interview with a John Smith.

The text of a release is usually (but not always) written in the style of a news story, with an eye-catching headline and text written standard journalistic inverted pyramid style. This style of news writing makes it easier for reporters to quickly grasp the message. Journalists are free to use the information verbatim, or alter it as they see fit. PR practitioners research and write releases that encourage as much "lifting" as possible. Many journalists believe it is unethical to copy from a press release-they believe it is a lapse of good judgement (for instance, a direct quote, as in:

Senator Smith said, "This is the most fiscally irresponsible bill that the Congress has passed since the Buy Everyone A Mercedes Act." In this case, a journalist may copy the quote verbatim into the story, although ethical reporters prefer to try soliciting an individual quote from the speaker before filing their story). Public relations professionals believe that press releases and other collateral material aid a journalist's job, and it is the job of the journalist to decide whether or not reprinting material verbatim tells the real story.

Since press releases reflect their issuer's preferred interpretation or positive packaging of a story, journalists are often skeptical of their contents. The level of skepticism depends on what the story is and who's telling it. Newsrooms receive so many press releases that, unless it is a story that the media are already paying attention to, a press release alone often isn't enough to catch a journalist's attention.

With the advent of modern electronic media and new technology, press releases now have equivalents in these media_video news releases and audio news releases. However, many television stations are hesitant to use VNR's that appear canned and are not newsworthy.

A New Kind of Press Release-"optimized" for the Internet

The advent of the Internet has ushered in a new kind of press release known as an optimized press release. Unlike conventional press releases of yore, written for journalists' eyes only, in hopes the editor or reporter would find the content compelling enough to turn it into print or electronic news coverage, the optimized press release is posted on an on-line news portal. Here the writer carefully selects keywords or keyword phrases relevant to the press release contents. If written skilfully, the press release can rank highly in searches on Google News, Yahoo or MSN News (or the many other minor news portals) for the chosen keyword phrases.

Readers of optimized press releases constitute far more than journalists. In the days before news search engines, a press release would have landed only in the hands of a news reporter or an editor who would make the decision about whether the content warranted news coverage. Although the news media is always privy to on-line press releases in the search engines, most readers are end-users. Optimized press releases circumvent the mainstream media which is formerly-but no longer-the gatekeeper of the news.

Lobby Groups

Lobby groups are established to influence government policy, corporate policy, or public opinion. These groups claim to represent a particular interest. When a lobby group hides its true purpose and support base it is known as a front group.

Spin

In public relations, spin is a sometimes pejorative term signifying a heavily biased portrayal in one's own favour of an event or situation. While traditional public relations may also rely on creative presentation of the facts, "spin" often, though not always, implies disingenuous, deceptive and/or highly manipulative tactics. Politicians are often accused of spin by commentators and political opponents, when they produce a counter argument or position.

The term is borrowed from ball sports such as cricket, where a spin bowler may impart spin on the ball during a delivery so that it will curve through the air or bounce in an advantageous manner.

The techniques of "spin" include:

- Selectively presenting facts and quotes that support one's position (cherry picking)
- Non-denial denial
- Phrasing in a way that assumes unproven truths

- Euphemisms to disguise or promote one's agenda
- Ambiguity
- Skirting
- Rejecting the validity of hypotheticals
- Appealing to internal policies

Another spin technique involves careful choice of timing in the release of certain news so it can take advantage of prominent events in the news. A famous reference to this practice occurred when British Government press officer Jo Moore used the phrase It's now a very good day to get out anything we want to bury, (widely paraphrased or misquoted as "It's a good day to bury bad news"), in an email sent on September 11, 2001. The furor caused when this email was reported in the press eventually caused her to resign.

Spin Doctor

Skilled practitioners of spin are sometimes called "spin doctors", though probably not to their faces unless it is said facetiously. It is the PR equivalent of calling a writer a "hack". Perhaps the most well-known person in the UK often described as a "spin doctor" is Alastair Campbell, who was involved with Tony Blair's public relations between 1994 and 2003, and also played a controversial role as press relations officer to the British and Irish Lions rugby side during their 2005 tour of New Zealand.

The American radio and television talk-show host Bill O'Reilly, who is often considered a spokesman for neoconservatism, has called his television show The O'Reilly Factor "The No Spin Zone", emphasizing his own purported dislike of the phenomenon.

Some other American talk and radio-show hosts and commentators, such as Keith Olbermann, who maintains an on-going "feud with Bill O'Reilly", and who himself has been tagged with being more liberal in his views, mock O'Reilly's epithet "no spin zone" suggesting his own avoidance of "spin" to be just another instance of spin from "the other side". (Olbermann frequently labels O'Reilly as "The Worst Person in the World" in one of his segments on his own show Countdown, which airs at the same time as The O'Reilly Factor on rival cable network MSNBC.) Such commentators on politics, despite their prominent roles in mainstream-media journalism, which purports to maintain objectivity, at times and sometimes even often seem engaged in the very phenomenon of spin that they deride.

Many such commentators and their featured on-air media consultants, commonly termed "talking heads" or pundits, come to programs on radio, television, and in publishing from prior professional careers in public relations and politics, sometimes even as former political campaign directors or speech writers for political figures; for those who do, mastering the "art" of spin has already been an important part of their past work experience, and it may lead not only to their acute understanding and critique of the phenomenon but also to their supreme ability to continue practising it in ever-more subtle ways.

State-run media in many countries also engage in spin by selectively allowing news stories that are favourable to the government while censoring anything that could be considered critical. They may also use propaganda to indoctrinate or actively influence citizens' opinions.

Other

- Publicity events, pseudo-events, photo or publicity stunts
- The talk show circuit. A PR spokesperson (or his/her client) "does the circuit" by being interviewed on television and radio talk shows with audiences that the client wishes to reach.
- Books and other writings

- After a PR practitioner has been working in the field for a while, he or she accumulates a list of contacts in the media and elsewhere in the public affairs sphere. This "Rolodex" becomes a prized asset, and job announcements sometimes even ask for candidates with an existing Rolodex, especially those in the media relations area of PR.
- Direct communication (carrying messages directly to constituents, rather than through the mass media) with, e.g., newsletters-in print and e-letters.
- Collateral literature, traditionally in print and now predominantly as web sites.
- Speeches to constituent groups and professional organizations; receptions; seminars, and other events; personal appearances.
- The slang term for a PR practitioner or publicist is a "flack."

3

The Process of Public Relations

Scott Cutlip, Allen Center and Glen Broom describe the public relations process in four steps (1994). The first step is "Defining Public Relations Problems," usually in terms of a "situational analysis," or what public relations professionals call a SWOT analysis (strengths, weaknesses, opportunities, threats). According to Cutlip, Center and Broom, this should answer the question, "What's happening now?" The next step in the public relations process is "Planning and Programming," where the main focus is "strategy," Cutlip, Center and Broom argue that this step should answer the question "What should we do and say, and why?" The third step in the public relations process is "Taking action and Communicating," also known as "Implementation;" this step should answer the question "How and when do we do and say it?" The final step in Cutlip, Center and Broom's Four-Step Public Relations Process is "Evaluating The Program," making a final "assessment," which should answer the question "How did we do," this is where public relations professionals make a final analysis of the success of their campaign or communication.

Another process model by Sheila C. Crifasi (2000) uses the acronym "ROSIE" to define a five-step process of "Research, Objectives, Strategies, Implementation and Evaluation (See Media evaluation)." Using another acronym, "ROPES," Dr. Kathleen S. Kelly explains a five-step process through "Research, Objectives, Program, Evaluation and

Stewardship." Wilcox, Ault, Agee and Cameron (2002) define the public relations process through four steps of "Research, Action (Program Planning), Communication and Evaluation." Center and Jackson (1995) define the process of public relations through four steps: "Fact-finding and data gathering; Planning and programming; Action and communication; Evaluation."

People who are professionals in public relations use different methods for analyzing the results of their work such as focus groups, surveys, and one-on-one interviews. These same methods are used in defining what medium of communication will be used in the process of strategy and what tools will be used in relaying the message, such as press releases, brochures, Web sites, media packs, video news releases, news conferences and in-house publications.

On-line PR is increasingly gaining prominence and credibility in its own right, as PR pros use new technologies including the Internet to further client goals. On-line PR pros should be fluent in blogging, link-building, social media sites such as Digg, and SEO/SEM practices.

POLITICS AND CIVIL SOCIETY

Defining the Opponent

A tactic used in political campaigns is known as "defining one's opponent". Opponents can be candidates, organizations and other groups of people.

In the 2004 US presidential campaign, George W. Bush defined John Kerry as a "flip-flopper," among other characterizations, which were widely reported and repeated by the media, particularly the conservative media. Similarly, George H.W. Bush characterized Michael Dukakis as weak on crime (the Willie Horton ad) and as hopelessly liberal ("a card-carrying member of the ACLU"). In 1996, President Bill Clinton seized upon opponent Bob Dole's promise to take America back to a simpler time, promising in contrast to "build a bridge to the 21st century." This painted Dole as a person who was somehow opposed to progress.

In the debate over abortion, self-titled pro-choice groups, by virtue of their name, defined their opponents as "anti-choice", while self-titled pro-life groups refer to their opponents as "pro-abortion" or "anti-life". See Power word.

More recently, opponents of same-sex marriage in the U.S. have declared that their opponents are not the gay couples suing for the right to marry in various state courts, but rather the judges who rule in their favour. They are now calling them "activist judges," implying that they impose their personal beliefs instead of objectively interpreting the law. This sidesteps the thorny issue of making millions of gay people an "enemy," and instead focuses attention on the much smaller judiciary, who all Americans can ostensibly agree should be prevented from being "activists" on the bench.

Managing Language

If a politician or organization can use an apt phrase in relation to an issue, such as in interviews or news releases, the news media will often repeat it verbatim, without questioning the aptness of the phrase. This perpetuates both the message and whatever preconceptions might underlie it.

"New Deal" became a description of President Franklin D. Roosevelt's anti-Depression economic plans, and "states' rights/state sovereignty" became near-code words for anti-civil rights legislation.

Recent examples include: "death tax" for estate tax, "racial preferences" for affirmative action, "faith-based" instead of religious, "climate change" for global warming, and "partial-birth abortion", a non-medical term used to describe the types of abortion performed late-term. The phrase "weapons of mass destruction" became extremely common in the lead-up the 2003 invasion of Iraq, often with little comment on what specific weapons those might be.

ENTERTAINMENT AND CELEBRITY

Playing up Weaknesses

Celebrities tend to be fans of the dictum "any publicity is good publicity". If a celebrity says or does something embarrassing, he or she will often turn it into a strength and make it part of his or her "image." This tactic is used just as much with favourable situations as much as with unfavourable ones.

A current (2004) example involves the entertainer Jessica Simpson, who gained nationwide prominence when she wondered aloud on a reality show if "Chicken of the Sea"-brand tuna fish was actually chicken or tuna, garnering her a reputation for being slow-witted. But by the summer of 2004, she was being paid to endorse a brand of breath mints called "Liquid Ice." In the product's television commercial, Simpson replicates her earlier confusion by debating whether the mint is really liquid or ice. So although she was previously ridiculed, she (and her advisers) turned her nationwide embarrassment into a lucrative endorsement deal.

Branching Out

As Oscar Wilde said in The Picture of Dorian Gray, the only thing worse than being talked about is not to be talked about at all. Many celebrities seem to take this truism to heart, because when their popularity (and income) wane, they take on new projects that attract media attention. Considering that a celebrity's celebrity is a brand unto itself, many celebrities are under constant pressure to "reinvent" themselves, as a prophylactic against obscurity.

A current trend among celebrities is the transformation of musicians, comedians, and almost every other sort of performer into children's book authors. Madonna, Jay Leno, Billy Crystal, Jerry Lawler, Keith Hernandez, Ricky Gervais and several other celebrities have recently written children's books, accompanied by much media coverage.

A more traditional way of branching out is the celebrity restaurant. This is especially common among professional athletes, whose time in the spotlight is often limited by the physical demands of their jobs. Basketball player Michael Jordan opened a restaurant in Chicago, and singer Britney Spears opened an ill-fated eatery in New York which closed a few months later.

Male celebrities like Tim Robbins, Sean Penn and Charlton Heston seem to gravitate toward politics, although some female celebrities, such as Susan Sarandon and Barbra Streisand, also become strong political voices.

Younger female celebrities on the other hand are often drawn into the fashion world. Hotel heiress Paris Hilton recently announced that she was starting her own line of jewellery, and Jennifer Lopez has started a line of clothing. And fading star Elizabeth Taylor launched a fragrance called "White Diamonds" several years ago, bringing renewed interest from the media. Britney Spears also kept herself in the public eye when she had her secretive marriage to Kevin Federline and bore his child. Although neither topic has to do with her career, audiences seemed to be just as intrigued to know about her personal life.

Some celebrities have also entered the world of self promotion by establishing other business ventures. St. Louis rapper Nelly's Vokal for men and Applebottoms for Women and Ludacris's "Disturbing the Peace" record company are both examples of celebrities taking public relations into their own hands.

Front Groups

Many of the techniques used by PR firms are drawn from the institutions and practices of democracy itself. Persuasion, advocacy, and education are instruments through which individuals and organizations are entitled to express themselves in a free society, and many public relations practitioners are engaged in practices that are widely considered as beneficial, such as publicizing scientific research, promoting charities, raising awareness of public health concerns and other issues in civil society.

One of the most controversial practices in public relations is the use of front groups-organizations that purport to serve a public cause while actually serving the interests of a client whose sponsorship may be obscured or concealed. The creation of front groups is an example of what PR practitioners sometimes term the third party technique-the art of "putting your words in someone else's mouth." PR Watch, a non-profit organization that monitors PR activities it considers to be deceptive, has published numerous examples of this technique in practice. Critics of the public relations industry, such as PR Watch, have contended that Public Relations involves a "multi-billion dollar propaganda-for-hire industry" that "concoct[s] and spin[s] the news, organize[s] phoney 'grassroots' front groups, sp[ies] on citizens, and conspire[s] with lobbyists and politicians to thwart democracy.".

Instances of the use of front groups as a PR technique have been documented in many industries. Coal mining corporations have created environmental groups that contend that increased CO_2 emissions and global warming will contribute to plant growth and will be beneficial, trade groups for bars have created and funded citizens' groups to attack anti-alcohol groups, and tobacco companies have created and funded citizens' groups to advocate for tort reform and to attack personal injury lawyers.

Current issues in ethical and social arenas have been brought to the attention of people from all strata of the population when it was found that more than one journalist with a platform had received money from a Public Relations firm for espousing a certain point of view.

Localization of Public Relations

One should also pay attention to the impact of globalization has on the form and styles of public relations.

We need to be aware of the localization of public relations in different regions and countries. An excellent example would be the Chinese public relations field. The early development of public relations in China is reflected in the 1989 national award winning TV series "Public Relations Ladies" written by Kuang Jianren. The concept of public relations was made-known through this original work, which also revealed the economic reform and social political changes in China in the 1980s.

Public Relations in Fiction and on TV

- Absolutely Fabulous (1992-2004) is a British sitcom written by and starring Jennifer Saunders with Joanna Lumley.
- Absolute Power (2000-) is a British comedy series, set in the offices of Prentiss McCabe, a fictional public relations company in London.
- Wag the Dog (1997), an American movie about a PR-consultant (Robert De Niro) that teams up with a movie-producer (Dustin Hoffman) to cover up a presidential sex scandal by creating a fictional war to divert the media.
- Thank You for Smoking (1994), an American satirical novel by Christopher Buckley, about a shyster PR-Consultant/tobacco-lobbyist (Nick Naylor) during the 1990s. It was later adapted into a movie of the same title in 2006.
- Everyone Worth Knowing (2005), a novel by The Devil Wears Prada author Lauren Weisberger, is a novel about a twenty-something woman who gets a job in public relations and is introduced to the New York City night life.

4

The Propaganda

Introduction

Propaganda [from modern Latin: 'Propaganda Fide', literally "propagating the faith"] is a concerted set of messages aimed at influencing the opinions or behaviour of groups of people. Instead of impartially providing information, propaganda can present accurate facts, but does so selectively to produce deliberately misleading information, or loaded messages, whether essentially truthful or not, in order to produce an emotional rather than rational response to the message that is being presented. While emotional appeal over reason is the essential defining element of propaganda, the desired result is a change of the cognitive narrative of the subject by the target audience.

Etymology

In 1622, shortly after the start of the Thirty Years' War, Pope Gregory XV founded the Congregatio de Propaganda Fide ("Congregation for Spreading the Faith"), a committee of Cardinals with the duty of overseeing the propagation of Christianity by missionaries sent to Catholic countries. Therefore, the term itself originates with this Byzantine Catholic Sacred Congregation for the Propagation of the Faith (sacra congregatio christiano nomini propagando or, briefly, propaganda fide), the department of the pontifical administration charged with the spread of Catholicism and with the regulation of ecclesiastical affairs in non-Catholic countries (mission territory). The Latin stem propagand- conveys a sense of "that which ought to be spread". Originally the term was not intended to refer to misleading information. The modern sense dates from World War I, when the term evolved to be mainly associated with politics.

Purpose of Propagandism

The aim of propagandism is to influence people's opinions or behaviours actively, rather than merely to communicate the facts about something. For example, propaganda might be used to gather either support or disapproval of a certain position, rather than to simply present the position, or to try to convince people to buy something, rather than to simply let them know there is some thing on the market.

What separates propagandism from "normal" communication is in ways by which the message attempts to shape opinion or behaviour, which are often subtle and insidious among other characteristics. For example, propagandism is often presented in a way that attempts to deliberately evoke a strong emotion, especially by suggesting illogical (or non-intuitive) relationships between concepts or objects (for instance between a "good" car and an attractive woman or a sex symbol).

An appeal to one's emotions is, perhaps, a more obvious, and more common propagandism method than those utilized by some other more subtle and insidious forms. For instance, propagandism may be transmitted indirectly or implicitly, through an ostensibly fair and balanced debate or argument. This can be done to great effect in conjunction with a broadly targeted, broadcast news format. In such a setting, techniques like, "red herring", and other ploys (such as Ignoratio elenchi), are often used to divert the audience from a critical issue, while the intended message is suggested through indirect means.

This sophisticated type of diversion utilizes the appearance of lively debate within what is actually a carefully focused spectrum, to generate and justify deliberately conceived assumptions. This technique avoids the distinctively biased appearance of one sided rhetoric, and works by presenting a contrived premise for an argument as if it were a universally accepted and obvious truth, so that the audience naturally assumes it to be correct.

By maintaining the range of debate in such a way that it appears inclusive of differing points of view, so as to suggest fairness and balance, the suppositions suggested become accepted as fact. Here is such an example of a hypothetical situation in which the opposing viewpoints are supposedly represented: the hawk (see: hawkish) says, "we must stay the course", and the dove says, "The war is a disaster and a failure", to which the hawk responds, "In war things seldom go smoothly and we must not let setbacks affect our determination", the dove retorts, "setbacks are setbacks, but failures are failures."

In this example, the actual validity of the war is not discussed and is never in contention. One may naturally assume that the war was not fundamentally wrong, but just the result of miscalculation, and therefore, an error, instead of a crime. Thus, by maintaining the appearance of equitable discourse in such debates, and through continuous inculcation, such focused arguments succeed in compelling the audience to logically deduce that the presuppositions of debate are unequivocal truisms of the given subject.

The method of propaganda is essential to the word's meaning as well. A message does not have to be untrue to qualify as propaganda. The message in modern propaganda is often not blatantly untrue. But even if the message conveys only "true" information, it will generally contain partisan bias and fail to present a complete and balanced consideration of the issue. Another common characteristic of propaganda is volume (in the sense of a large amount). For example, a propagandist may seek to influence opinion by attempting to get a message heard in as many places as possible, and as often as possible. The intention of this approach is to (a) reinforce an idea through repetition, and (b) exclude or "drown out" any alternative ideas.

In English, the word "propaganda" now carries strong negative (as well as political, mainly) connotations, although it has not always done so. It was formerly common for political organizations, as it had started to be for the advertising and public relations industry, to refer to their own material as propaganda. Because of the negative connotations the word has gained, today it is uncommon to admit producing propaganda, although opposing parties sometimes accuse each other of producing propaganda. Other languages, however, do not necessarily regard the term as derogatory and hence usage may lead to misunderstanding in communications with non-native English speakers.

Public relations pioneer Edward L. Bernays in his classic studies eloquently describes propaganda as the purpose of communications. In Crystallizing Public Opinion, for example, he dismisses the semantic differentiations ("Education is valuable, commendable, enlightening, instructive. Propaganda is insidious, dishonest, underhanded, misleading.") and instead concentrates on purposes. He writes (p. 212), "Each of these nouns carries with it social and moral implications... The only difference between 'propaganda' and 'education,' really, is in the point of view. The advocacy of what we believe in is education. The advocacy of what we don't believe in is propaganda."

The reason propaganda exists and is so widespread is because it serves various social purposes, necessary ones, often popular yet potentially corrupting. Many institutions such as media, private corporations and government itself are literally propaganda-addicts, co-dependent on each other and the fuelling influence of the propaganda system that they help create and maintain. Propagandists have an advantage through knowing what they want to promote and to whom, and although they often resort to various two-way forms of communication this is done to make sure their one-sided purposes are achieved.

TYPES OF PROPAGANDA

A 1947 comic book published by the Catechetical Guild Educational Society warning of "the dangers of a Communist takeover".

Propaganda shares techniques with advertising and public relations. Advertising and public relations can be thought of as propaganda that promotes a commercial product or shapes the perception of an organization, person or brand, though in post-World War II usage the word "propaganda" more typically refers to political or nationalist uses of these techniques or to the promotion of a set of ideas, since the term had gained a pejorative meaning, which commercial and government entities couldn't accept. The refusal phenomenon was eventually to be seen in politics itself by the substitution of 'political marketing' and other designations for 'political propaganda'.

Propaganda was often used to influence opinions and beliefs on religious issues, particularly during the split between the Catholic Church and the Protestants. Propaganda has become more common in political contexts, in particular to refer to certain efforts sponsored by governments, political groups, but also often covert interests. In the early 20th century the term propaganda was also used by the founders of the nascent public relations industry to describe their activities. This usage died out around the time of World War II, as the industry started to avoid the word, given the pejorative connotation it had acquired.

Literally translated from the Latin gerundive as "things which must be disseminated", in some cultures the term is neutral or even positive, while in others the term has acquired a strong negative connotation. The connotations of the term "propaganda" can also vary over time. For example, in

Portuguese and some Spanish language speaking countries, particularly in the Southern Cone, the word "propaganda" usually refers to the most common manipulative media-"advertising".

In English, "propaganda" was originally a neutral term used to describe the dissemination of information in favour of any given cause. During the 20th century, however, the term acquired a thoroughly negative meaning in western countries, representing the intentional dissemination of often false, but certainly "compelling" claims to support or justify political actions or ideologies.

This redefinition arose because both the Soviet Union and Germany's government under Hitler admitted explicitly to using propaganda favouring, respectively, communism and fascism, in all forms of public expression. As these ideologies were antipathetic to liberal western societies, the negative feelings toward them came to be projected into the word "propaganda" itself.

> *"Propaganda is neutrally defined as a systematic form of purposeful persuasion that attempts to influence the emotions, attitudes, opinions, and actions of specified target audiences for ideological, political or commercial purposes through the controlled transmission of one-sided messages (which may or may not be factual) via mass and direct media channels. A propaganda organization employs propagandists who engage in propagandism-the applied creation and distribution of such forms of persuasion."-R.A. Nelson, A Chronology and Glossary of Propaganda in the United States, 1996*

Roderick Hindery argues that propaganda exists on the political left, and right, and in mainstream centrist parties. Hindery further argues that debates about most social issues can be productively revisited in the context of asking "what is or is not propaganda?" Not to be overlooked is the link between propaganda, indoctrination, and terrorism/ counterterrorism. She argues that threats to destroy are often as socially disruptive as physical devastation itself.

Propaganda also has much in common with public information campaigns by governments, which are intended to encourage or discourage certain forms of behaviour (such as wearing seat belts, not smoking, not littering and so forth). Again, the emphasis is more political in propaganda. Propaganda can take the form of leaflets, posters, TV and radio broadcasts and can also extend to any other medium. In the case of the United States, there is also an important legal (imposed by law) distinction between advertising (a type of overt propaganda) and what the Government Accountability Office (GAO), an arm of the United States Congress, refers to as "covert propaganda."

Journalistic theory generally holds that news items should be objective, giving the reader an accurate background and analysis of the subject at hand. On the other hand, advertisements evolved from the traditional commercial advertisements to include also a new type in the form of paid articles or broadcasts disguised as news. These generally present an issue in a very subjective and often misleading light, primarily meant to persuade rather than inform. Normally they use only subtle propaganda techniques and not the more obvious ones used in traditional commercial advertisements. If the reader believes that a paid advertisement is in fact a news item, the message the advertiser is trying to communicate will be more easily "believed" or "internalized."

Such advertisements are considered obvious examples of "covert" propaganda because they take on the appearance of objective information rather than the appearance of propaganda, which is misleading. Federal law specifically mandates that any advertisement appearing in the format of a news item must state that the item is in fact a paid advertisement. The Bush Administration has been criticized for allegedly producing and disseminating covert propaganda in the form of television programs, aired in the United States, which appeared to be legitimate news broadcasts and did not include any information signifying that the programs were not generated by a private-sector news source.

Propaganda, in a narrower use of the term, connotates deliberately false or misleading information that supports or furthers a political (but not only) cause or the interests of those with power. The propagandist seeks to change the way people understand an issue or situation for the purpose of changing their actions and expectations in ways that are desirable to the interest group. Propaganda, in this sense, serves as a corollary to censorship in which the same purpose is achieved, not by filling people's minds with approved information, but by preventing people from being confronted with opposing points of view. What sets propaganda apart from other forms of advocacy is the willingness of the propagandist to change people's understanding through deception and confusion rather than persuasion and understanding. The leaders of an organization know the information to be one sided or untrue, but this may not be true for the rank and file members who help to disseminate the propaganda.

More in line with the religious roots of the term, it is also used widely in the debates about new religious movements (NRMs), both by people who defend them and by people who oppose them. The latter pejoratively call these NRMs cults. Anti-cult activists and countercult activists accuse the leaders of what they consider cults of using propaganda extensively to recruit followers and keep them. Some social scientists, such as the late Jeffrey Hadden, and CESNUR affiliated scholars accuse ex-members of "cults" who became vocal critics and the anti-cult movement of making these unusual religious movements look bad without sufficient reasons.

Propaganda is a powerful weapon in war; it is used to dehumanize and create hatred toward a supposed enemy, either internal or external, by creating a false image in the mind. This can be done by using derogatory or racist terms, avoiding some words or by making allegations of enemy atrocities. Most propaganda wars require the home population to feel the enemy has inflicted an injustice, which may be fictitious or may be based on facts. The home population must also decide that the cause of their nation is just.

Propaganda is also one of the methods used in psychological warfare, which may also involve false flag operations. The term propaganda may also refer to false information meant to reinforce the mindsets of people who already believe as the propagandist wishes. The assumption is that, if people believe something false, they will constantly be assailed by doubts. Since these doubts are unpleasant (see cognitive dissonance), people will be eager to have them extinguished, and are therefore receptive to the reassurances of those in power. For this reason propaganda is often addressed to people who are already sympathetic to the agenda. This process of reinforcement uses an individual's predisposition to self-select "agreeable" information sources as a mechanism for maintaining control.

Propaganda can be classified according to the source and nature of the message. White propaganda generally comes from an openly identified source, and is characterized by gentler methods of persuasion, such as standard public relations techniques and one-sided presentation of an argument. Black propaganda is identified as being from one source, but is in fact from another. This is most commonly to disguise the true origins of the propaganda, be it from an enemy country or from an organization with a negative public image. Grey propaganda is propaganda without any identifiable source or author.

In scale, these different types of propaganda can also be defined by the potential of true and correct information to compete with the propaganda. For example, opposition to white propaganda is often readily found and may slightly discredit the propaganda source. Opposition to grey propaganda, when revealed (often by an inside source), may create some level of public outcry. Opposition to black propaganda is often unavailable and may be dangerous to reveal, because public cognizance of black propaganda tactics and sources would undermine or backfire the very campaign the black propagandist supported.

Propaganda may be administered in insidious ways. For instance, disparaging disinformation about the history of certain groups or foreign countries may be encouraged or tolerated in the educational system. Since few people actually double-check what they learn at school, such disinformation will be repeated by journalists as well as parents, thus reinforcing the idea that the disinformation item is really a "well-known fact", even though no one repeating the myth is able to point to an authoritative source. The disinformation is then recycled in the media and in the educational system, without the need for direct governmental intervention on the media. Such permeating propaganda may be used for political goals: by giving citizens a false impression of the quality or policies of their country, they may be incited to reject certain proposals or certain remarks or ignore the experience of others. See also: black propaganda, marketing, advertising

Techniques

Common media for transmitting propaganda messages include news reports, government reports, historical revision, junk science, books, leaflets, movies, radio, television, and posters. In the case of radio and television, propaganda can exist on news, current-affairs or talk-show segments, as advertising or public-service announce "spots" or as long-running advertorials. Propaganda campaigns often follow a strategic transmission pattern to indoctrinate the target group. This may begin with a simple transmission such as a leaflet dropped from a plane or an advertisement. Generally these messages will contain directions on how to obtain more information, via a web site, hot line, radio program, et cetera (as it is seen also for selling purposes among other goals). The strategy intends to initiate the individual from information recipient to information seeker through reinforcement, and then from information seeker to opinion leader through indoctrination.

A number of techniques which are based on social psychological research are used to generate propaganda. Many of these same techniques can be found under logical fallacies, since propagandists use arguments that, while sometimes convincing, are not necessarily valid.

Some time has been spent analyzing the means by which propaganda messages are transmitted. That work is important but it is clear that information dissemination strategies only become propaganda strategies when coupled with propagandistic messages. Identifying these messages is a necessary prerequisite to study the methods by which those messages are spread.

Below are a number of techniques for generating propaganda:

- *Ad Hominem*: A Latin phrase which has come to mean attacking your opponent, as opposed to attacking their arguments.
- *Appeal to Authority*: Appeals to authority cite prominent figures to support a position, idea, argument, or course of action. Appealing to authority is a valid type of argument if the authority being appealed to is a noted expert in the area in question. However, if an argument, say on a medical issue, is supported by appending the support of a political or military authority, it may not be a valid form of argument.
- *Appeal to Fear*: Appeals to fear seek to build support by instilling anxieties and panic in the general

population, for example, Joseph Goebbels exploited Theodore Kaufman's Germany Must Perish! to claim that the Allies sought the extermination of the German people.

- *Appeal to Prejudice*: Using loaded or emotive terms to attach value or moral goodness to believing the proposition. For example, the phrase: "Any hard-working taxpayer would have to agree that those who do not work, and who do not support the community do not deserve the community's support through social assistance."
- *Argumentum ad Nauseam*: This argument approach uses tireless repetition of an idea. An idea, especially a simple slogan, that is repeated enough times, may begin to be taken as the truth. This approach works best when media sources are limited and controlled by the propagator.
- *Bandwagon*: Bandwagon and "inevitable-victory" appeals attempt to persuade the target audience to join in and take the course of action that "everyone else is taking."
    * *Inevitable Victory*: invites those not already on the bandwagon to join those already on the road to certain victory. Those already or at least partially on the bandwagon are reassured that staying aboard is their best course of action.
    * *Join the Crowd*: This technique reinforces people's natural desire to be on the winning side. This technique is used to convince the audience that a program is an expression of an irresistible mass movement and that it is in their best interest to join.
- *Black-and-White Fallacy:* Presenting only two choices, with the product or idea being propagated as the better choice. (e.g., "You are either with us, or you are with the enemy")

- *Beautiful People*: The type of propaganda that deals with famous people or depicts attractive, happy people. This makes other people think that if they buy a product or follow a certain ideology, they too will be happy or successful.
- *Big Lie: The* repeated articulation of a complex of events that justify subsequent action. The descriptions of these events have elements of truth, and the "big lie" generalizations merge and eventually supplant the public's accurate perception of the underlying events. After World War I the German Stab in the back explanation of the cause of their defeat became a justification for Nazi re-militarization and revanchist aggression.
- *Common man*: The "'plain folks'" or "common man" approach attempts to convince the audience that the propagandist's positions reflect the common sense of the people. It is designed to win the confidence of the audience by communicating in the common manner and style of the target audience. Propagandists use ordinary language and mannerisms (and clothe their message in face-to-face and audiovisual communications) in attempting to identify their point of view with that of the average person. For example, a propaganda leaflet may make an argument on a macroeconomic issue, such as unemployment insurance benefits, using everyday terms: "given that the country has little money during this recession, we should stop paying unemployment benefits to those who do not work, because that is like maxing out all your credit cards during a tight period, when you should be tightening your belt."
- *Demonizing the Enemy*: Making individuals from the opposing nation, from a different ethnic group, or those who support the opposing viewpoint appear to be subhuman (e.g., the Vietnam War-era term "gooks"

for Viet Cong soldiers), worthless, or immoral, through suggestion or false accusations.

- *Direct Order*: This technique hopes to simplify the decision making process by using images and words to tell the audience exactly what actions to take, eliminating any other possible choices. Authority figures can be used to give the order, overlapping it with the Appeal to authority technique, but not necessarily. The Uncle Sam "I want you" image is an example of this technique.
- *Euphoria*: The use of an event that generates euphoria or happiness, or using an appealing event to boost morale. Euphoria can be created by declaring a holiday, making luxury items available, or mounting a military parade with marching bands and patriotic messages.
- *Disinformation*: The creation or deletion of information from public records, in the purpose of making a false record of an event or the actions of a person or organization, including outright forgery of photographs, motion pictures, broadcasts, and sound recordings as well as printed documents.
- *Flag-waving*: An attempt to justify an action on the grounds that doing so will make one more patriotic, or in some way benefit a group, country, or idea. The feeling of patriotism which this technique attempts to inspire may not necessarily diminish or entirely omit one's capability for rational examination of the matter in question.
- *Glittering Generalities*: Glittering generalities are emotionally appealing words applied to a product or idea, but which present no concrete argument or analysis. A famous example is the campaign slogan "Ford has a better idea!"
- *Intentional Vagueness*: Generalities are deliberately vague so that the audience may supply its own

interpretations. The intention is to move the audience by use of undefined phrases, without analyzing their validity or attempting to determine their reasonableness or application. The intent is to cause people to draw their own interpretations rather than simply being presented with an explicit idea. In trying to "figure out" the propaganda, the audience foregoes judgment of the ideas presented. Their validity, reasonableness and application may still be considered.

- *Obtain Disapproval or Reductio ad Hitlerum*: This technique is used to persuade a target audience to disapprove of an action or idea by suggesting that the idea is popular with groups hated, feared, or held in contempt by the target audience. Thus if a group which supports a certain policy is led to believe that undesirable, subversive, or contemptible people support the same policy, then the members of the group may decide to change their original position.
- *Oversimplification*: Favourable generalities are used to provide simple answers to complex social, political, economic, or military problems.
- *Quotes out of Context*: Selective editing of quotes which can change meanings. Political documentaries designed to discredit an opponent or an opposing political viewpoint often make use of this technique.
- *Rationalization*: Individuals or groups may use favourable generalities to rationalize questionable acts or beliefs. Vague and pleasant phrases are often used to justify such actions or beliefs.
- *Red herring/Chewbacca Defense*: Presenting data or issues that, while compelling, are irrelevant to the argument at hand, and then claiming that it validates the argument.

- *Repetition*: This type of propaganda deals with a jingle or word that is repeated over and over again, thus getting it stuck in someones head, so they can buy the product. The "Repetition" method has been described previously.
- *Scapegoating*: Assigning blame to an individual or group, thus alleviating feelings of guilt from responsible parties and/or distracting attention from the need to fix the problem for which blame is being assigned.
- *Slogans*: A slogan is a brief, striking phrase that may include labelling and stereotyping. Although slogans may be enlisted to support reasoned ideas, in practice they tend to act only as emotional appeals. Opponents of the US's invasion and occupation of Iraq use the slogan "blood for oil" to suggest that the invasion and its human losses was done to access Iraq's oil riches. On the other hand, "hawks" who argue that the US should continue to fight in Iraq use the slogan "cut and run" to suggest that it would be cowardly or weak to withdraw from Iraq. Similarly, the names of the military campaigns, such as "enduring freedom" or "just cause", may also be regarded to be slogans, devised to influence people.
- *Stereotyping or Name Calling or Labelling*: This technique attempts to arouse prejudices in an audience by labelling the object of the propaganda campaign as something the target audience fears, hates, loathes, or finds undesirable. For instance, reporting on a foreign country or social group may focus on the stereotypical traits that the reader expects, even though they are far from being representative of the whole country or group; such reporting often focuses on the anecdotal.

- *Testimonial*: Testimonials are quotations, in or out of context, especially cited to support or reject a given policy, action, program, or personality. The reputation or the role (expert, respected public figure, etc.) of the individual giving the statement is exploited. The testimonial places the official sanction of a respected person or authority on a propaganda message. This is done in an effort to cause the target audience to identify itself with the authority or to accept the authority's opinions and beliefs as its own. See also, damaging quotation
- *Transfer*: Also known as Association, this is a technique of projecting positive or negative qualities (praise or blame) of a person, entity, object, or value (an individual, group, organization, nation, patriotism, etc.) to another to make the second more acceptable or to discredit it. It evokes an emotional response, which stimulates the target to identify with recognized authorities. Often highly visual, this technique often utilizes symbols (for example, the Swastika used in Nazi Germany, originally a symbol for health and prosperity) superimposed over other visual images. An example of common use of this technique in America is for the President's image to be overlayed with a swastika by his opponents.
- *Unstated Assumption*: This technique is used when the propaganda concept that the propagandist intends to transmit would seem less credible if explicitly stated. The concept is instead repeatedly assumed or implied.
- *Virtue Words*: These are words in the value system of the target audience which tend to produce a positive image when attached to a person or issue. Peace, happiness, security, wise leadership, freedom, "The Truth", etc. are virtue words. In counties such as the U.S. religiosity is seen as a virtue, making associations to this quality effectively beneficial.

PROPAGANDA MODELS

Herman and Chomsky's Propaganda Model

The propaganda model is a theory advanced by Edward S. Herman and Noam Chomsky that alleges systemic biases in the mass media and seeks to explain them in terms of structural economic causes.

> *"The 20th century has been characterized by three developments of great political importance: the growth of democracy, the growth of corporate power, and the growth of corporate propaganda as a means of protecting corporate power against democracy."*

First presented in their 1988 book Manufacturing Consent: the Political Economy of the Mass Media, the propaganda model views the private media as businesses selling a product-readers and audiences (rather than news)-to other businesses (advertisers). The theory postulates five general classes of "filters" that determine the type of news that is presented in news media: Ownership of the medium; Medium's funding sources; Sourcing; Flak; and Anti-communist ideology.

The first three (ownership, funding, and sourcing) are generally regarded by the authors as being the most important. Although the model was based mainly on the characterization of United States media, Chomsky and Herman believe the theory is equally applicable to any country that shares the basic economic structure and organizing principles which the model postulates as the cause of media biases. After the disintegration of the Soviet Union, Chomsky stated that the new filter replacing communism would be terrorism and Islam.

Ross' Epistemic Merit Model

The epistemic merit model is a method for understanding propaganda conceived by Sheryl Tuttle Ross and detailed in her 2002 article for the Journal of Aesthetic Education entitled

"Understanding Propaganda: The Epistemic Merit Model and Its Application to Art". Ross developed the Epistemic merit model due to concern about narrow, misleading definitions of propaganda. She contrasted her model with the ideas of Pope Gregory XV, the Institute for Propaganda Analysis, Alfred Lee, F.C. Bartlett, and Hans Speier. Insisting that each of their respective discussions of propaganda are too narrow, Ross proposed her own definition.

To appropriately discuss propaganda, Ross argues that one must consider a threefold communication model: that of Sender-Message-Receiver. "That is... propaganda involve[s]... the one who is persuading (Sender) [who is] doing so intentionally, [the] target for such persuasion (Receiver) and [the] means of reaching that target (Message)." There are four conditions for a message to be considered propaganda. Propaganda involves the intention to persuade. As well, propaganda is sent on behalf of a sociopolitical institution, organization, or cause. Next, the recipient of propaganda is a socially significant group of people. Finally, propaganda is an epistemical struggle to challenge other thoughts.

Ross claims that it is misleading to say that propaganda is simply false, or that it is conditional to a lie, since often the propagandist believes in what he/she is propagandizing. In other words, it is not necessarily a lie if the person who creates the propaganda is trying to persuade you of a view that they actually hold. "The aim of the propagandist is to create the semblance of credibility." This means that they appeal to an epistemology that is weak or defective.

False statements, bad arguments, immoral commands as well as inapt metaphors (and other literary tropes) are the sorts of things that are epistemically defective... Not only does epistemic defectiveness more accurately describe how propaganda endeavours to function... since many messages are in forms such as commands that do not admit to truth-values, [but it] also accounts for the role context plays in the workings of propaganda.

Throughout history those who have wished to persuade have used art to get their message out. This can be accomplished by hiring artists for the express aim of propagandizing or by investing new meanings to a previously nonpolitical work. Therefore, Ross states, it is important to consider "the conditions of its making [and] the conditions of its use."...

HISTORICAL CONTEXT OF PROPAGANDA

Ancient Propaganda

Propaganda has been a human activity as far back as reliable recorded evidence exists. The Behistun Inscription (c. 515 BC) detailing the rise of Darius I to the Persian throne, can be seen as an early example of propaganda. The Arthashastra written by Chanakya (c. 350-283 BC), a professor of political science at Takshashila University and a prime minister of the Maurya Empire, discusses propaganda in detail, such as how to spread propaganda and how to apply it in warfare. His student Chandragupta Maurya (c. 340-293 BC), founder of the Maurya Empire, employed these methods during his rise to power. The writings of Romans such as Livy (c. 59 BC-17 AD) are considered masterpieces of pro-Roman statist propaganda.

19th and 20th Centuries

Gabriel Tarde's Laws of Imitation (1890) and Gustave Le Bon's The Crowd: A Study of the Popular Mind (1897) were two of the first codifications of propaganda techniques, which influenced many writers afterward, including Sigmund Freud. Hitler's Mein Kampf is heavily influenced by Le Bon's theories. Journalist Walter Lippman, in Public Opinion (1922) also worked on the subject, as well as psychologist Edward Bernays, a nephew of Freud, early in the 20th century.

During World War I, Lippman and Bernays were hired by then United States President, Woodrow Wilson, to participate in the Creel Commission, the mission of which was to sway popular opinion in favour of entering the war, on the side of the United Kingdom. The Creel Commission provided themes for speeches by "four-minute men" at public functions, and also encouraged censorship of the American press. The Commission was so unpopular that after the war, Congress closed it down without providing funding to organize and archive its papers.

The war propaganda campaign of Lippman and Bernays produced within six months such an intense anti-German hysteria as to permanently impress American business (and Adolf Hitler, among others) with the potential of large-scale propaganda to control public opinion. Bernays coined the terms "group mind" and "engineering consent", important concepts in practical propaganda work.

The current public relations industry is a direct outgrowth of Lippman's and Bernays' work and is still used extensively by the United States government. For the first half of the 20th century Bernays and Lippman themselves ran a very successful public relations firm. World War II saw continued use of propaganda as a weapon of war, both by Hitler's propagandist Joseph Goebbels and the British Political Warfare Executive, as well as the United States Office of War Information.

In the early 2000s, the United States government developed and freely distributed a video game known as America's Army. The stated intention of the game is to encourage players to become interested in joining the U.S. Army. According to a poll by I for I Research, 30% of young people who had a positive view of the military said that they had developed that view by playing the game.

Russian Revolution

Russian revolutionaries of the 19th and 20th centuries distinguished two different aspects covered by the English term propaganda. Their terminology included two terms: agitation, and propaganda, see agitprop (agitprop is not, however, limited to the Soviet Union, as it was considered, before the October Revolution, to be one of the fundamental activity of any Marxist activist; this importance of agit-prop in Marxist theory may also be observed today in Trotskyist circles, who insist on the importance of leaflet distribution).

Soviet propaganda meant dissemination of revolutionary ideas, teachings of Marxism, and theoretical and practical knowledge of Marxist economics, while agitation meant forming favourable public opinion and stirring up political unrest. These activities did not carry negative connotations (as they usually do in English) and were encouraged. Expanding dimensions of state propaganda, the Bolsheviks actively used transportation such as trains, aircraft and other means.

Josef Stalin's regime built the largest fixed-wing aircraft of the 1930s, Tupolev ANT-20, exclusively for this purpose. Named after the famous Soviet writer Maxim Gorky who had recently returned from fascist Italy, it was equipped with a powerful radio set called "Voice from the sky", printing and leaflet-dropping machinery, radio stations, photographic laboratory, film projector with sound for showing movies in flight, library, etc. The aircraft could be disassembled and transported by railroad if needed. The giant aircraft set a number of world records.

Nazi Germany

Most propaganda in Germany was produced by the Ministry for Public Enlightenment and Propaganda (Propagandaministerium, or "Promi", its German abbreviation). Joseph Goebbels was placed in charge of this ministry shortly after Hitler took power in 1933. All journalists, writers, and artists were required to register with one of the Ministry's subordinate chambers for the press, fine arts, music, theatre, film, literature, or radio.

The Nazis believed in propaganda as a vital tool in achieving their goals. Adolf Hitler, Germany's Führer, was impressed by the power of Allied propaganda during World War I and believed that it had been a primary cause of the collapse of morale and revolts in the German home front and Navy in 1918 (see also: Dolchstoßlegende). Hitler would meet nearly every day with Goebbels to discuss the news and Goebbels would obtain Hitler's thoughts on the subject; Goebbels would then meet with senior Ministry officials and pass down the official Party line on world events. Broadcasters and journalists required piior approval before their works were disseminated. Along with posters, the Nazis produced a number of films and books to spread their beliefs.

Cold War Propaganda

The United States and the Soviet Union both used propaganda extensively during the Cold War. Both sides used film, television, and radio programming to influence their own citizens, each other, and Third World nations. The United States Information Agency operated the Voice of America as an official government station. Radio Free Europe and Radio Liberty, which were in part supported by the Central Intelligence Agency, provided grey propaganda in news and entertainment programs to Eastern Europe and the Soviet Union respectively. The Soviet Union's official government station, Radio Moscow, broadcast white propaganda, while Radio Peace and Freedom broadcast grey propaganda. Both sides also broadcast black propaganda programs in periods of special crises.

In 1948, the United Kingdom's Foreign Office created the IRD (Information Research Department) which took over from wartime and slightly post-war departments such as the Ministry of Information and dispensed propaganda via various media such as the BBC and publishing.

The ideological and border dispute between the Soviet Union and People's Republic of China resulted in a number of cross-border operations. One technique developed during this period was the "backwards transmission", in which the radio program was recorded and played backwards over the air. (This was done so that messages meant to be received by the other government could be heard, while the average listener could not understand the content of the program.)

When describing life in capitalist countries, in the US in particular, propaganda focused on social issues such as poverty and anti-union action by the government. Workers in capitalist countries were portrayed as "ideologically close". Propaganda claimed rich people from the US derived their income from weapons manufacturing, and claimed that there was substantial racism or neo-fascism in the US.

When describing life in Communist countries, western propaganda wanted created an image of a people held hostage by governments that brainwash their people. The West also created a fear of the East, by depicting an aggressive Soviet Union. In the Americas, Cuba served as a major source and a target of propaganda from both black and white stations operated by the CIA and Cuban exile groups. Radio Habana Cuba, in turn, broadcast original programming, relayed Radio Moscow, and broadcast The Voice of Vietnam as well as alleged confessions from the crew of the USS Pueblo.

George Orwell's novels Animal Farm and Nineteen Eighty-Four are virtual textbooks on the use of propaganda. Though not set in the Soviet Union, these books are about totalitarian regimes in which language is constantly corrupted for political purposes. These novels were, ironically, used for explicit propaganda. The CIA, for example, secretly commissioned an animated film adaptation of Animal Farm in the 1950s with small changes to the original story to suit its own needs.

Revolution in Central and Eastern Europe

During the democratic revolutions of 1989 in Central and Eastern Europe the propaganda poster was important weapon in the hand of the opposition. Brave printed and hand-made political posters appeared on the Berlin Wall, on the statue of St. Wenseslas in Prague and around the unmarked grave of Imre Nagy in Budapest and the role of them was indispensable for the democratic change.

The Afghan War

In the 2001 invasion of Afghanistan, psychological operations tactics were employed to demoralize the Taliban and to win the sympathies of the Afghan population. At least six EC-130E Commando Solo aircraft were used to jam local radio transmissions and transmit replacement propaganda messages. Leaflets were also dropped throughout Afghanistan, offering rewards for Osama bin Laden and other individuals, portraying Americans as friends of Afghanistan and emphasizing various negative aspects of the Taliban. Another shows a picture of Mohammed Omar in a set of crosshairs with the words "We are watching." This Technique has been shown to be rather ineffective in terms of long term opinions change given current political and social conditions in Afghanistan.

The US Air Force can use cluster bombs to deliver leaflets. The LBU-30 clusterbomb is designed to allow an aircraft to deliver leaflets to a target area while minimizing wind drift.

The Iraq War

During the 2003 invasion of Iraq, the Iraqi Information Minister Mohammed Saeed al-Sahaf repeatedly claimed Iraqi forces were decisively winning every battle. Even up to the overthrow of the Iraqi government at Baghdad, he maintained that the United States would soon be defeated, in contradiction with all other media. Due to this, he quickly became a cult figure in the West, and gained recognition on the website WeLoveTheIraqiInformationMinister.com The Iraqis, misled by his propaganda, on the other hand, were shocked when instead Iraq was defeated.

In November 2005, The Chicago Tribune and the Los Angeles Times, alleged that the United States military had manipulated news reported in Iraqi media in an effort to cast a favourable light on its actions while demoralizing the insurgency. Lt. Col. Barry Johnson, a military spokesman in Iraq, said the program is "an important part of countering misinformation in the news by insurgents", while a spokesman for former Defense Secretary Donald H. Rumsfeld said the allegations of manipulation were troubling if true.

The Department of Defense has confirmed the existence of the program. The New York Times published an article about how the Pentagon has started to use contractors with little experience in journalism or public relations to plant articles in the Iraqi press. These articles are usually written by US soldiers without attribution or are attributed to a non-existent organization called the "International Information Center." Planting propaganda stories in newspapers was done by both the Allies and Central Powers in the First World War and the Axis and Allies in the Second; this is the latest version of this technique.

Children and Propaganda

Of all the potential targets for propaganda, children are the most vulnerable because they are the most unprepared for the critical reasoning and contextual comprehension required to determine whether a message is propaganda or not. Children's vulnerability to propaganda is rooted in developmental psychology. The attention children give their environment during development, due to the process of developing their understanding of the world, will cause them to absorb propaganda indiscriminately. Also, children are highly imitative: studies by Albert Bandura, Dorothea Ross and Sheila A. Ross in the 1960s indicated that children are susceptible to filmed representations of behaviour. Therefore television is of particular interest in regard to children's vulnerability to propaganda.

Another vulnerability of children is the theoretical influence that their peers have over their behaviour.

According to Judith Rich Harris's group-socialization theory, children learn the majority of what they do not receive paternally, through genes, from their peer groups. The implication then is that if peer-groups can be indoctrinated through propaganda at a young age to hold certain beliefs, the group will self-regulate the indoctrination, since new members to the group will adapt their beliefs to fit the group's.

To a degree, socialization, formal education, and standardized television programming can be seen as using propaganda for the purpose of indoctrination. Schools that utilize dogmatic, frozen world-views, often resort to propagandist curricula that indoctrinate children. The use of propaganda in schools was highly prevalent during the 1930s and 1940s in Germany, as well as in Stalinist Russia.

In Nazi Germany, the education system was thoroughly co-opted to indoctrinate the German youth with anti-Semitic ideology. This was accomplished through the National Socialist Teachers' Union, of which 97% of all German teachers were members in 1937. It encouraged the teaching of "racial theory." Picture books for children such as Don't Trust A Fox in A Green Meadow Or the Word of A Jew, The Poisonous Mushroom, and The Poodle-Pug-Dachshund-Pincher were widely circulated (over 100,000 copies of Don't Trust A Fox... were circulated during the late 1930s) and contained depictions of Jews as devils, child molesters, and other morally charged figures. Slogans such as "Judas the Jew betrayed Jesus the German to the Jews" were recited in class. The following is an example of a propagandistic math problem recommended by the National Socialist Essence of Education.

AESTHETICIZATION AS PROPAGANDA

Aesthetics is the branch of philosophy that studies the nature of beauty and the moral value of art, so aestheticization as propaganda is the process of presenting any form of behaviour considered dangerous or threatening as an acceptable means of promoting a political aim, for example violence that may involve injury or death.

Overview

Each culture formulates mechanisms for considering the acceptability of behaviour and its outcomes. For example, utilitarianism may take the ontological view that the greatest good will be achieved for the largest number of people if violence is used in particular situations, i.e. morality as utility is expressed in the form of a cost-benefit analysis.

Propaganda is a method used to influence the discourse by offering alternative constructions of the paradigms of social acceptability, no matter whether the tests are described as moral, ethical, pragmatic or otherwise. Anything that is said or shown through the mass media can be true or false, sincere or dishonest, but propaganda is distinguishable from conventional types of political or religious communication.

In communication theory it is described as framing in that the words or images selected are packaged to sell an interpretation of events to a specific audience. If the framing is successful, the paradigms will expand to admit the proposed or actual violence into the class of events considered acceptable (or, in some cases, desirable).

The Aestheticization of Violence for Political Purposes

Though many tools are available for political purposes, the threat or use of violence attracts those of a more proactive disposition as the simplest way to resolve any conflict or achieve any ends, because its strategies are well-known and weapons easily obtained. When asked to identify alternative nonviolent techniques, people find it difficult to visualise effective methods; moreover, sceptics can quickly raise moral and practical dilemmas to complicate any set of choices until violence appears the easiest option.

Thus, this topic is relevant across a spectrum of causes from those disagree about social or commercial practices within their local community, to those unhappy with the political regime in their own country, to those who believe that another country is a threat.

Nevertheless, a person or group wishing to use violence as a strategy must overcome objections from both prospective supporters and the other interested parties. No cause will prosper until the majority agrees with the justifications offered for the decision to use force, because all who adopt aggressive strategies require emotional and logistical support from the local community for success.

Hence, the aestheticization process is used to direct the audience's interpretation of events by shifting the values of the lexical words used to minimise consideration of the moral, ethical or other costs. In Nineteen Eighty-Four, George Orwell proposed that the means to achieve complete control of people's minds or their ability to think rationally about the issues at stake is to invent a new language, more primitive and less articulate than current "oldspeak". That is the intention of aestheticization. It seeks to subvert the rationality of the current paradigms through doublespeak and goodthink, and to persuade the majority that the use of violence in the particular context is not merely necessary or expedient, but just and glorious in the prosecution of higher ideals.

Whether the use of violence is or is not justifiable is irrelevant for these purposes. The sole interest lies in the mechanism for the transfer of the particular use from the paradigm of unacceptable into the paradigm of acceptable. In contemporary terms, this brings semiotics into a position of prominence both to set the frame and to deconstruct it.

An Example of Semiotic Analysis

In January, 2003, the U.S. implemented a battle plan based on a concept developed at the National Defense University. Called "Shock and Awe" (see Americanism), its stated purpose was the psychological destruction of the enemy's will to fight rather than the physical destruction of his military forces. The choice of name is revealing, even at a denotative level.

Shock refers to the surprise and distress caused by events and, when associated with battles, means the violent interaction of individuals or groups as they join in combat. Meanwhile, awe is an overwhelming sense of wonder or admiration that may, to a greater or lesser extent, be associated with fear. But, at a connotative level, the use of the words is intended to fulfil several distinct aims:

In reality, the army may be going to kill large numbers of people, both combatant and non-combatant. These words are not the actions but they represent them at a symbolic level. Analysis shows that the words fall within the paradigm of lexical words signifying the emotional responses to external stimuli: responses that can only be experienced by those who are alive. The intended implication is that enemy soldiers and civilians will be so disoriented by the display of power that they will simply surrender rather than face the threatened injury or death. Hence, the enemy casualty count will be low and the immediate gains will significantly outweigh the moral, ethical or other costs of the enterprise.

All warfare involves death and destruction on a scale that may be shocking to the sensibilities of the ordinary person, so what is the value of these words? Applying the commutation test, substitutes for "shock" might be: excitement, impact, and surprise, as opposed to: scare, trauma, and upset.

The substitutes for "awe" might be: admiration, reverence and wonder, as opposed to fear, horror, and terror. Both words are capable of signifying less appealing qualities but, by setting them in a conjoined relationship, the expectation is that they will both be given the same value. The sui generis rule applies so that second and subsequent words in a conjoined sequence define the class. Evaluating the substitutes for "shock", the degree of match as synonyms seems reasonably adjacent and the balance of connotation can be considered balanced.

This would give the word "shock" a relatively neutral value. Since the preponderance of connotation to "awe" is positive (the negative substitutes are less directly synonymous), the relationship in the phrase is intended to invoke values suggesting a certain degree of magnificence in the technology and the manner of its delivery. Not only those on the receiving end are expected to experience awe: all external observers may be impressed by this display of power, and, perhaps, feel not a little afraid-a useful general propaganda gain.

The connotation of the word awe tends to refer to unequal power relationships, e.g. a beginner may be in awe of the skills of a professional, an ordinary mortal is in awe of a deity, etc. The implication is that this war is such an asymmetrical contest that the enemy might just as well give up before the battle is joined with such an overwhelmingly superior force.

Figurative usages provide what the semiotician Roland Barthes called a "pleasure of the text" (1970), i.e. the pleasurable reaction produced by a clever arrangement of signs. So figurative words are more memorable than literal words, particularly when used in unexpected contexts. Using this phrase in the otherwise literal context of declaring the opening of violent hostilities is incongruous and that contextualisation has made the phrase memorable, effectively displacing all the imagery of imminent death and destruction that might otherwise have dominated.

Monosyllabic words wield considerable rhetorical might: they are short, punchy, and memorable. Through the careful mixing of short and long words, the impact provided by the short words stands out against the rhythmic flow provided by long words. Rhetorical theory maintains that any proposition can be expressed in a variety of ways.

Hence, when persuasion is the overriding goal, the rhetorical perspective suggests that the manner in which a statement is expressed may be more important than its propositional content. In this instance, the repetition of two sounds, a binary pair of semi-onomatopoeic words, produces hyperbole. Whether written or spoken with an appropriate intonation and body language, the phrase is memorable and serves its aestheticization function.

Propaganda of the Deed

Propaganda of the deed (or propaganda by the deed, from the French propagande par le fait) is a concept of anarchist origin, which appeared towards the end of the 19th century, that promoted physical violence against political enemies as a way of inspiring the masses and catalyzing revolution.

There is no single definition of propaganda of the deed. Propaganda of the deed may take many forms, but in most cases utilizes violence which is often euphemized as "direct action". Due in particular to this concept of "propaganda of the deed", the anarchist movement has often been represented as violent and "terrorist", beginning with several bombings and assassinations at the end of the 19th century. This image has stuck, anarchists are still today often caricatured as wild-eyed fanatics with a stereotypical fuse-lit bomb.

"Direct action" however must not necessarily involve violence; it may imply non-violent but illegal activity, legal alternatives to political participation, or violent actions ranging from bombings to explicit acts of murder and assassination. Peter Kropotkin described the effects of a single action. "By actions which compel general attention, the new idea seeps into people's minds and wins converts. One such act may, in a few days, make more propaganda than thousands of pamphlets."

ANARCHIST ORIGINS

Definitions of Propaganda of the Deed

An early proponent of propaganda by the deed was the Italian revolutionary Carlo Pisacane (1818-1857), who wrote in his "Political Testament" (1857) that "ideas spring from deeds and not the other way around." Mikhail Bakunin (1814-1876), in his "Letters to a Frenchman on the Present Crisis" (1870) stated that "we must spread our principles, not with words but with deeds, for this is the most popular, the most potent, and the most irresistible form of propaganda."

The phrase "propaganda by the deed" was popularized by the French anarchist Paul Brousse (1844-1912). In his article of that name, published in the August 1877 Bulletin of the Jura Federation, he cited the 1871 Paris Commune, a workers' demonstration in Berne provocatively using the socialist red flag, and the Benevento uprising in Italy as examples of "propaganda by the deed."

Some anarchists, such as Johann Most, advocated publicizing violent acts of retaliation against counter-revolutionaries because "we preach not only action in and for itself, but also action as propaganda." Most was an early influence on American anarchists Emma Goldman and Alexander Berkman. Berkman attempted propaganda by the deed when he tried in 1892 to kill industrialist Henry Clay Frick following the shooting deaths of several striking workers.

By the 1880s, the slogan "propaganda of the deed" had begun to be used both within and outside of the anarchist movement to refer to individual bombings, regicides and tyrannicides. However, as soon as 1887, important figures in the anarchist movement distanced themselves from such individual acts. Peter Kropotkin thus wrote that year in Le Révolté that "it is an illusion to believe that a few kilos of dynamite will be enough to win against the coalition of exploiters". A variety of anarchists advocated the abandonment of these sorts of tactics in favour of collective revolutionary action, for example through the trade union movement. The anarcho-syndicalist, Fernand Pelloutier, argued in 1895 for renewed anarchist involvement in the labour movement on the basis that anarchism could do very well without "the individual dynamiter."

State repression (including the infamous 1894 French lois scélérates) of the anarchist and labour movements following the few successful bombings and assassinations may have contributed to the abandonment of these kinds of tactics, although reciprocally state repression, in the first place, may have played a role in these isolated acts. The destructuration of the French socialist movement, divided into many groups, and, following the suppression of the 1871 Paris Commune, the execution and exile of many communards to penal colonies, favoured individualist political expression and acts.

Other theorists advocating propaganda of the deed included the Italian anarchists Luigi Galleani and Errico Malatesta. Malatesta described "propaganda by the deed" as violent communal insurrections that were meant to ignite the imminent revolution. For the German anarchist Gustav Landauer "propaganda of the deed" meant the creation of libertarian social forms and communities that would inspire others to transform society. In "Weak Statesmen, Weaker People," he wrote that the state is not something "that one can smash in order to destroy. The state is a relationship between human beings... one destroys it by entering into other relationships"

In 1886, French anarchist Clément Duval achieved a form of propaganda of the deed stealing 15 000 francs from the mansion of a Parisian socialite, beforc accidentally setting the house on fire. Caught two weeks later, he was dragged from the court crying "Long live anarchy!", and condemned to death. His sentence was later commuted to hard labour on Devil's Island, French Guiana. In the anarchist paper

Révolte, Duval famously declared that, "Theft exists only through the exploitation of man by man... when Society refuses you the right to exist, you must take it... the policeman arrested me in the name of the Law, I struck him in the name of Liberty".

Propaganda of the deed is also related to illegalism, an anarchist philosophy that developed primarily in France, Italy, Belgium, and Switzerland durir.g the early 20th century as an outgrowth of anarchist individualism. The illegalists openly embraced criminality as a lifestyle. Influenced by theorist Max Stirner's concept of "egoism", the illegalists broke from anarchists like Clément Duval and Marius Jacob who justified theft with a theory of la reprise individuelle (Eng: individual reclamation). Instead, the illegalists argued that their actions required no moral basis-illegal acts were taken not in the name of a higher ideal, but in pursuit of one's own desires. France's Bonnot Gang was the most famous group to embrace illegalism.

Theorization of propaganda of the deed as a way to accelerate the coming of revolution.

Propaganda of the deed thus included stealing (in particular bank robberies-named "expropriations" or "revolutionary expropriations" to finance the organization), rioting and general strikes which aimed at creating the conditions of an insurrection or even a revolution. These acts were justified as the necessary counterpart to state repression. As sociologist Max Weber had argued, the state has the "monopoly on the legitimate use cf physical force", or, in Karl Marx's words, the state was only the repressive apparatus of the bourgeois class. Propaganda by the deed, including assassinations (sometimes involving bombs, named in French "machines infernales"-"hellish machines", usually made with bombs, sometimes only several guns assembled together), were thus legitimized by part of the anarchist movement and the First International as a valid means to be used in class struggle. The predictable state responses to these actions were supposed to display to the people the inherently repressive nature of the bourgeois state. This would in turn bolster the revolutionary spirit of the people, leading to the overthrow of the state. This is the basic formula of the cycle protests-repression-protests, which in specific conditions may lead to an effective state of insurrection.

This cycle has been observed during the 1905 Russian Revolution or in Paris in May 1968. However, it failed to achieve its revolutionary objective on the vast majority of occasions, thus leading to the abandonment by the vast majority of the anarchist movement of such bombings. However, the state never failed in its repressive response, enforcing various lois scélérates which usually involved tough clampdowns on the whole of the labour movement. These harsh laws, sometimes accompanied by the proclamation of the state of exception, progressively led to increased criticism among the anarchist movement of assassinations. The role of several agents provocateurs and the use of deliberate strategies of tension by governments, using false flag terrorist actions, work to discredit this violent tactic in the eyes of most socialist libertarians.

Regicides and other Assassinations

Numerous heads of state were assassinated between 1881 and 1914 by members of the libertarian socialist movement. Regicides were for obvious reasons celebrated as popular victory over counter-revolutionary forces, which remained strong a century after the 1789 French Revolution. The first assassinations were carried out by Russian anarchists, which would lead to the creation of the term of "nihilism". For example, U.S. President McKinley's assassin Leon Czolgosz claimed to have been influenced by anarchist and feminist Emma Goldman. This was in spite of Goldman's disavowal of any association with him, his registered membership in the Republican Party, and never having belonged to an anarchist organization. Bombings were associated in the media with anarchists because international terrorism arose during this time period with the widespread distribution of dynamite. This image remains to this day. This perception was enhanced by events such as the 1886 Haymarket Riot, where anarchists were blamed for throwing a bomb at police who came to break up a public meeting in Chicago, Illinois.

List of assassinated important figures and other propaganda by the deed acts:

- April 4, 1866. A bullet shot at Alexander II by Dmitry Karakozov misses narrowly. It is the first of many such assassination attempts by revolutionaries. He fails and is hanged, with four others, on September 3.
- January 1878. Vera Zasulich shot and wounded General Theodore Trepov, military governor of St. Petersburg, after he had ordered the flogging of political prisoner Arkhip Bogoliubov (real name: Alexander Emelianov). At her trial a sympathetic jury found her not guilty.
- 1878. Failed assassination attempt against Alfonso XII of Spain.
- May 11, 1878. Failed assassination attempt of Max Hödel against Kaiser Wilhelm I.
- June 2, 1878. Failed assassination attempt of Karl Nobiling against the Kaiser.
- August 1878. Sergey Kravchinsky stabs to death General Nikolai Mezentsov, head of the Tsar's secret police, in response to the execution of Ivan Kovalsky.
- February 1879. Grigori Goldenberg shoots to death the Governor of Kharkov, Prince Dmitri Kropotkin.
- April 1879. Alexander Soloviev shoots at Alexander II. This second attempt on the royal's life also fails.

- November 1879. Lev Bronstein attempts, without success, to blow up the Imperial railway carriage. His more famous nephew of the same name goes on to become a founding father of the Soviet Union.
- 1880. Stepan Khalturin's successfully blows up of part of the Winter Palace-8 soldiers killed, 45 wounded. Referring to the 1862 invention of dynamite, historian Benedict Anderson observes that "Nobel's invention had now arrived politically."
- March 1 (Julian calendar) 1881. Tsar Alexander II is killed in a bomb-blast by Narodnaya Volya.
- July 23, 1892. Alexander Berkman tries to kill Henry Clay Frick in retaliation for the killing of workers by Pinkerton detectives during the Homestead Steel Strike.
- December 9, 1893. Auguste Vaillant throws a nail bomb in the French National Assembly, killing nobody and injuring one. He is then sentenced to death and executed by the guillotine on February 4, 1894, shouting "Death to bourgeois society and long live anarchy!" (A mort la société bourgeoise et vive l'anarchie!). During his trial, Auguste Vaillant declared that he hadn't intended to kill anybody, but only to injure several deputies in retaliation against the execution of Ravachol, who had engaged himself in four bombings.
- December 11 and 18, 1893. Vote of the French lois scélérates.
- February 12, 1894. Emile Henry set a bomb in Café Terminus, killing one and injuring twenty. During his trial, he declares: "There is no innocent bourgeois". This act is one of the rare exceptions to the rule that propaganda of the deed targets only specific powerful individuals.

- June 24, 1894. Italian anarchist Caserio stabs to death French president Sadi Carnot to avenge Auguste Vaillant and Emile Henry. Caserio is then executed by guillotine on August 15.
- August 8, 1897. Michele Angiolillo assassinates Spanish Prime minister Cánovas, who had been a key figure in the 1874 overthrow of the Republic, helping the Bourbon monarchy back to the throne.
- September 10, 1898. Luigi Lucheni stabs to death with a needle file Elisabeth of Bavaria, Empress consort of Austria and Queen consort of Hungary due to her marriage to Emperor Franz Joseph.
- July 29, 1900. Gaetano Bresci shoots dead Umberto I of Italy, avenging the Bava-Beccaris massacre in Milan.
- September 6, 1901. Leon Czolgosz shoots at point-blank range on U.S. president William McKinley, killing him. He is then killed by electrocution on October 29 (Czolgosz' anarchist status is a matter of debate. He attended anarchist meetings and read anarchist texts yet was a registered Republican).
- October 1902. Gennaro Rubino attempts to murder Leopold II of Belgium.
- 1904. Yegor Sozonov throws a bomb into Russian minister of Interior von Plehve's carriage, killing him. Sozonov was a member of the Socialist-Revolutionary Combat Group, which was headed by agent provocateur Evno Azef.
- 1905. Socialist-Revolutionary Ivan Kalyayev uses a bomb to kill Duke Sergei Alexandrovich, fifth son of Tsar Alexander II.
- 31 May 1906. Catalan Anarchist Mateu Morral tries to kill Alfonso XIII of Spain and Victoria Eugenie of Battenberg after their wedding.

- February 1, 1908. Two Portuguese Republicans shoot King Carlos I and his son Luis Filipe, both of whom die. Manuel, the other son who had been injured in the assassination attempt, succeeded to Carlos I.
- September 14, 1911. Dmitri Bogrov shoots to death Russian prime minister Pyotr Stolypin.
- November 12, 1912. Anarchist Manuel Pardiñas kills Spanish Prime Minister José Canalejas in Madrid.
- 18 March 1913. Aleksander Schinas assassinates king George I of Greece.
- September 16, 1920. The Wall Street bombing kills 38 and wounds 400 in Manhattan's Financial District. Anarchists associated with Luigi Galleani are widely believed responsible although the crime remains officially unsolved.
- 8 March 1921. Three anarchists shoot Conservative politician Eduardo Dato Iradier dead from a motorcycle in Puerta de Alcalá, Madrid.
- 1922. Gustave Bouvet attempts to kill French president Alexandre Millerand.
- 1926. Sholom Schwartzbard assassinates Symon Petlura, head of the government-in-exile Ukrainian People's Republic, in Paris. After an eight-day trial, he is acquitted by the jury, who has been convinced of Schwartzbard's just cause: the core of his defence was that he was avenging the deaths of victims of pogroms organized by Symon Petlura.

LATER DEVELOPMENTS

The Abandonment of Bombings, and New Forms of Propaganda of the Deed

Propaganda of the deed, as a violent form of direct action involving bombings and targeted assassinations, was abandoned by the vast majority of the anarchist movement after World War I (1914-18) and the 1917 October Revolution. There are various causes for this, but important factors include state repression, the level of organization of the labour movement (in particular the new importance of anarcho-syndicalism in European Latin countries such as France, Italy and Spain) and the influence of the October Revolution. Although the Leninist thesis of an avant-garde party composed of professional revolutionaries didn't break that much with the Socialist-Revolutionary organization, it did make completely individual acts of propaganda of the deed less relevant. Despite this abandonment, the concept of propaganda of the deed remained popular in the anarchist movement, and thus influenced various social and cultural movements, including the Underground, during the 20th century.

For example, the concept of direct action itself continued to be central in the socialist libertarian movement, in particular in the anarcho-syndicalism movement through the concept of the "revolutionary strike" inspired by French theorist Georges Sorel's Reflections on Violence (1908). In the 1950s, the Situationist International's conception of creating "situations" may be related quite easily to propaganda of the deed (which is not surprising, given the influence of council communism on Guy Debord). The autonomist movement and urban guerrilla group then took on the concept in the 1970s. It is also during this period that the concept of culture jamming, Spaßguerilla, guerrilla communication and other kinds of non-violent and sometimes simultaneously artistic and political acts become popular as a new form of "direct action". The Living Theatre, in the 1970s, for example, mixed direct actions with an artistic intent, mixing, as did before them André Breton and the Surrealist movement, Arthur Rimbaud's "change life" with Karl Marx' XIth These on Feuerbach, "transform the world."

The importance of riots and rebellions in the creation of the conditions of an insurrection has never been abandoned, going through anarcho-syndicalism to autonomism and today's anti-globalization mediatic Black blocs. In the 2000s, a Swedish group called the Invisible Party carried on various direct actions which could be related to the tradition of the propaganda of the deed.

Urban Guerrilla Groups of the 1970s and the Autonomist Movement

The concept of "propaganda of the deed" received renewed attention in the 1970s-1980s, especially among "urban guerrilleros" and the Italian autonomist movement, which had a large part in the creation of the squatting and Social Center movement.

Since some of the most radical autonomist or other far-left activists engaged not only in direct action (stealing, squatting, bank robberies-called expropriations-etc.) but also in assassination and bombing, "propaganda of the deed" again became synonymous with terrorism. For example, the German Red Army Faction (RAF) kidnapped and murdered Hanns Martin Schleyer, who was president of the German Employer's Association and a former high-ranking SS member during the Third Reich, and targeted NATO centers.

The appearance in developed countries during the 1970s of militant leftist groups-such as the Red Brigades, the RAF or the less important French Action Directe-which (although they did not claim to be specifically anarchist, did engage in "propaganda of the deed")-, were part of a larger social movements. These included the autonomist movement in Italy, which practiced various types of "direct action" other than assassinations (in Italy, shootings in the legs was more often used). These new groups viewed their actions from a global point of view, in order to link them with "world struggles", such as the Vietnam War (1965-75) or with South American struggles against military juntas (see for example the RAF's actions against NATO and its ideological relations with Uruguayan Tupamaros). In Italy, the concept of a "strategy of tension" (strategia della tensione) directly carried on by far-right forces linked to the security forces was popular in extra-parliamentary leftist movements; its existence was proved after Italian Premier Giulio Andreotti's 1990 revelations concerning Gladio, a NATO stay-behind anti-communist organization, and the parliamentary inquiries into the bombings carried on during this period (1969 Piazza Fontana bombing, 1980 Bologna massacre, etc.).

Timeline of modern propaganda of the deed acts:

- April 20 1963. Gabriel Hudon, member of the Front de libération du Québec (FLB-National Liberation Front of Quebec) kills a night watchman in a bombing.
- May 1968. Riots in Paris. The New-York based group "Black Mask" becomes Up Against the Wall Motherfuckers and carry out propaganda of the deed, excluding assassinations and bombings.
- October 8, 1969. The U.S. group Weatherman's first event is to blow up a statue in Chicago, Illinois, dedicated to police casualties in the 1886 Haymarket Riot. The "Days of Rage" riots then occur in Chicago during four days. 287 Weatherman members are arrested, and one of them killed.
- December 6, 1969. Several Chicago Police cars parked in a Precinct parking lot at 3600 North Halsted Street, Chicago, are bombed. The Weather Underground Organization (WUO) later stated in their book Prairie Fire that they had perpetrated the explosion to protest the shooting deaths of the Illinois Black Panther Party leaders Fred Hampton and Mark Clark two days earlier by police officers.
- December 12, 1969. Piazza Fontana bombing (carried out by neofascists), beginning of Italy's years of lead and of the strategy of tension. In 1998, David Carrett, officer of the U.S. Navy, was put under investigations on charge of political and military espionage and his

participation in the Piazza Fontana bombing, among other events. Judge Guido Salvini also opened up a case against Sergio Minetto, Italian official for the US-NATO intelligence network, and pentito Carlo Digilio, who was suspected as a CIA informant. La Repubblica newspaper underlined that Carlo Rocchi, CIA's man at Milan, was surprised in 1995 searching for information concerning Operation Gladio, thus demonstrating that all was not over.

- 1970-1972. The British Angry Brigade group carries out at least 25 bombings (police numbers). Almost all property damage, although one person was slightly injured.
- June 1, 1970. The Montoneros, a Peronist left-wing group, kidnap and execute Pedro Aramburu, former dictator of Argentina, in retaliation for the June 1956 Leon Suarez massacre and the execution of Juan José Valle who had attempted a Peronist uprising against the military junta.
- September 12, 1970. The WUO helps Dr. Timothy Leary, LSD scientist, break out and escape from the California Men's Colony prison.
- October 8, 1970. Bombing of Marin County Courthouse (US) in retaliation for the killing of Black activists Jonathan Jackson, William Christmas, and James McClain.
- October 10, 1970. The Queens Courthouse is bombed to express support for the New York prison riots.
- October 14, 1970. The Harvard Center for International Affairs is bombed to protest the war in Vietnam.
- 1971. Foundation of the Black Liberation Army in the US. According to a Justice Department report on BLA activity, the Black Liberation Army was

suspected of involvement in over 60 incidents of violence between 1970 and 1976. Active until 1981.

- May 1972. Peteano attack. Although the Italian Red Brigades were accused of it, it would be later discovered that neofascist Vincenzo Vinciguerra, who maintained links with the military intelligence services, was actually responsible for it. After the Peteano attack, Vinciguerra escaped to Franquist Spain.
- September 25, 1973. Following the June 20, 1973 Ezeiza massacre on the day of Juan Perón's return from a 20 years-old exile, the Montoneros assassinate right-wing Peronist José Ignacio Rucci, secretary of the CGT and co-founder of the Triple A death squad.
- September 28, 1973. The ITT headquarters in New York and Rome, Italy are bombed in response to ITT's role in the September 11, 1973 Chilean coup.
- November 6, 1973. The U.S. group Symbionese Liberation Army (SLA) assassinates Oakland, California superintendent of schools Dr. Marcus Foster and badly wounded his deputy Robert Blackburn.
- 20 December, 1973. Operación Ogro: Basque nationalists from ETA blow Spanish Prime Minister Luis Carrero Blanco in his car in Madrid.
- July 1974. The Montoneros assassinate Arturo Mor Roig, former Interior minister of dictator Alejandro Lanusse (1971-1973).
- September 1974. The Montoneros kidnap two members of the Bunge and Born family, receiving as ransom $60 million in cash.
- September 11, 1974. Bombing of Anaconda Corporation (part of the Rockefeller Corporation) in retribution for Anaconda's involvement in Pinochet's coup exactly a year before.

- 1975. The German group Movement 2 June kidnaps Peter Lorenz, CDU candidate for mayor in Berlin, who is exchanged against four emprisonned comrades.
- December 1975. Greek organization Revolutionary Organization 17 November allegedly responsible of the assassination of CIA station chief in Athens Richard Welch. According to a December 2005 article by Kleanthis Grivas, journalist in Proto Thema, Sheepskin, Gladio's branch in Greece, was in fact behind the killing. US State Department denied Grivas' allegations in January 2006.
- January 28, 1975. Bombing of the U.S. State Department in response to escalation in Vietnam.
- April 21, 1975. The remaining members of the SLA rob the Crocker National Bank in Carmichael, California and kill Myrna Opsahl, a bank customer, in the process.
- September 1975. Bombing of the Kennecott Corporation in retribution for Kennecott's involvement in the Chilean coup two years prior.
- 1977. German Autumn: Hanns-Martin Schleyer, president of the German Employer's Association and a former high-ranking SS member, is kidnapped by the Red Army Faction (RAF), who tried to negotiate the liberation of the "first generation" of RAF members. Before the state's refusal to negotiate, the RAF highjacked the Lufthansa airplane Landshut with help from the Palestinian PFLP. On July 30, 1977, RAF members Brigitte Mohnhaupt, Susanne Albrecht and Christian Klar assassinate banker Jürgen Ponto, chairman of the Dresdner Bank board of directors, during a botched kidnapping attempt.
- May 1978. Italian prime minister Aldo Moro and leader of the Christian Democracy (DC) is murdered by the Second Red Brigades, led by Mario Moretti,

in obscure circumstances, involving a specific context of strategy of tension deliberately followed by Gladio, NATO's secret paramilitary "stay-behind" organization. Aldo Moro was kidnapped three months before, on the day the Italian Communist Party (PCI) was supposed to enter into the government aside the DC in virtu of the historic compromise.

- May 1, 1979. French group Action Directe carries out a machine gun attack on the employers' federation headquarters.
- 1980. Bologna massacre. Licio Gelli, head-master of Propaganda Due masonic lodge, would eventually be convicted of a sentence for investigation diversion, while two Italian intelligence agents are also involved. Two neofascists, members of the Nuclei Armati Rivoluzionari (NAR) are found directly responsible of the bombing (more than 80 killed), and charged with life-sentence in 1995.
- July 1980. Turkish left-wing organisation Dev Sol assassinates former Prime minister Nihat Erim.
- 15 September 1981 RAF member Brigitte Mohnhaupt take part in an assassination attempt on US General Frederick Kroesen using an RPG-7 anti-tank rocket. Kroesen only barely survived.
- May 30, 1982. The Canadian group Direct Action (aka "Squamish Five") set off a large bomb at an electricity transmission project. Four transformers were wrecked beyond repair, but no one was injured.
- 1984. Bomb-attacks of the Dutch organisation RaRa (Radical Anti-Racist Action) against the Van Heutsz monument (Van Heutzsch was the Dutch commander during the Aceh War).
- 1984-1985. Attacks on NATO and Belgian military infrastructures by the Communist Combatant Cells (CCC).

- 1985-1987: Dutch RaRa is responsible of several bomb-attacks on the Makro wholesale stores, which was active in South Africa.
- 1985. Action Directe assassinates René Audran, in charge of the state's arms-dealing.
- 1986. Georges Besse, CEO of Renault but before leader of Eurodif nuclear consortium (in which Iran had a 10% stake), is allegedly assassinated by Action Directe (although this thesis would be questioned, in particular by investigative journalist Dominique Lorentz).
- June 28, 1988. US naval and defense attachee in Greece William Nordeen's assassination is reinvidicated by the Revolutionary Organization 17 November.
- September 26, 1989. Assassination of Pavlos Bakoyannis, parliamentary leader of the liberal New Democracy party, by Greek group 17 November.
- 1991. Dutch Rara blow up the house of state secretary of justice Aad Kosto.
- 1993. Dutch Rara are responsible of bomb-attacks on the Dutch ministry of social affairs and employment.
- November 30, 1999. Black blocs destroy the storefronts of GAP, Starbucks, Old Navy, and other multinationals with retail locations in downtown Seattle during the anti-WTO demonstrations.
- 'June 8, 2000 Assassination of British military attache Stephen Saunders in Greece. Members of N-17 are arrested. In December 2005, Kleanthis Grivas, journalist in Proto Thema, claims that Sheepskin, Gladio's branch in Greece, was in fact behind the killing, along with the first violent act of N-17, Richard Welch CIA station chief's assassination in 1975. US State Department denied Grivas' allegations in January 2006.

- 2001. After the July Genoa G8 summit, the Publixtheatre Caravan, part of the No Border network, is accused of being part of a "criminal organization" called "Black blocs", although such "Black blocs" are not organized and only form themselves on a spontaneous manner during demonstrations, as in the older autonomist movement.
- May 6 2002. Dutch politician Pim Fortuyn was killed by vegan and left-wing activist Volkert van der Graaf.
- 2006. The Swedish Invisible Party announces its dissolving.

JUSTIFICATIONS FOR THE POLITICAL USE OF VIOLENCE

Anarchists and similar radicals often claim that their use of "political violence" is not terrorism, arguing that there is a fundamental difference between bombings carried out against a civilian population and targeted assassinations carried out against people in positions of political, military or economic power. They emphasize that many scholars define terrorism as the attempt to spread terror in the population through indiscriminate bombings, thus excluding anarchist propaganda of the deed from the definition of terrorism.

The use of political violence is understood by its proponents in the frame of a general conception of the state as the control apparatus of the "bourgeoisie", and of "class struggle" as a form of effective civil war. Thus, as anarchists often put it, "peace without justice isn't peace", but war between exploited and exploiters. In their eyes, this "social war" morally legitimizes the use of violence against broader "social violence." This view, of course, is not shared by pacifist libertarians. Rioting is thus justified as a means to enhance class consciousness and prepares the objective conditions for a popular uprising (Georges Sorel, 1906).

A heated controversy concerning the use of violence continues to take place inside the anarchist movement. Even those who are not opposed to the political use of violence for theoretical reasons (as pacifist anarchists are) may consider it unnecessary or strategically dangerous, in certain conditions. Many note that the events of 1970s showed clearly how terrorism may be used to influence politics in the frame of the "strategy of tension" by a state and its secret services, through agents provocateurs and false flag terrorist attacks. In Italy and other countries, the Years of lead led to reinforced anti-terrorism legislation, criticized by social activists as a new form of lois scélérates which were used to repress the whole of the socialist movement, not just militant groups. Many also note that the rare cases in which terrorism has achieved its revolutionary aims are mostly in the context of national liberation struggles, while the urban guerrilla movements have all failed (Gérard Chaliand).

5

Agenda-setting Theory

INTRODUCTION

The Agenda-setting theory,is the theory that the mass-news media have a large influence on audiences by their choice of what stories to consider newsworthy and how much prominence and space to give them. Agenda-setting theory's central axiom is salience transfer, or the ability of the mass media to transfer importance of items on their mass agendas to the public agendas.

HISTORY AND ORIGIN

The Media agenda is the set of issues addressed by media sources and the public agenda is the issues the public consider important (Miller, 2005). Agenda-setting theory was introduced in 1972 by Maxwell McCombs and Donald Shaw in their ground breaking study of the role of the media in 1968 presidential campaign in Chapel Hill, North Carolina.

The theory explains the correlation between the rate at which media cover a story and the extent that people think that this story is important. This correlation has repeatedly been shown to occur.

In the dissatisfaction of the magic bullet theory, many researchers began to study not how the media directly shaped individuals, but how the media shaped issues, particularly concerning political issues (Miller, 2005). Agenda-setting theory gave way that the press has some power, but individuals still are free to make their own decisions. Journalist Walter Lippman in his 1922 book Public Opinion raised the idea that the mass media create images of events in our minds, calling them "the pictures in our heads." Theodore White, a political analyst, studied how the media shaped political campaigns and concluded that the media shaped the way the public talk and think about political campaigns. Years later, Maxwell McCombs and Donald Shaw introduced agenda-setting theory in the Public Opinion Quarterly.

The theory was derived from their study that took place in Chapel Hill, NC, where the researchers surveyed 100 undecided voters during the 1968 presidential campaign on what they thought were key issues and measured that against the actual media content. The ranking of issues was almost identical. The conclusions matched their hypothesis: The mass media positioned the agenda for public opinion by emphasizing specific topics (Hamm, 1998). Subsequent research on agenda-setting theory provided evidence for the cause-and-effect chain of influence being debated by critics in the field. One particular study made leaps to prove the cause-effect relationship.

The study was conducted by Yale researchers, Shanto Iyengar, Mark Peters, and Donald Kinder. The researchers had three groups of subjects fill out questionnaires about their own concerns and then each group watched different evening news programs, each of which emphasized a different issue. After watching the news for four days, the subjects again filled out questionnaires and the issues that they rated as most important matched the issues they viewed on the evening news (Griffin, 2005). The study demonstrated a cause-and-effect relationship between media agenda and public agenda. Since the theory's conception, more than 350 studies have been performed to test the theory. The theory has evolved beyond the media's influence on the public's perceptions of issue salience to political candidates and corporate reputation (Carroll & McCombs, 2003).

IMPORTANT ASPECTS OF THE THEORY

Conceptual Model

Functions of Theory: The agenda-setting function has multiple components

1. Media Agenda-issues discussed in the media (newspapers, television, radio)
2. Public Agenda-issues discussed and personally relevant to members of the public
3. Policy Agenda-issues that policy makers consider important (legislators)
4. Corporate Agenda-issues that big business and corporations consider important (corporate)

These four agendas are interrelated. Two basic assumptions underlie most research on agenda-setting: (1) The press and the media do not reflect reality, they filter and shape it; (2) media concentration on a few issues and subjects leads the public to perceive those issues as more important than other issues.

Characteristics

Research has focused on characteristics of audience, the issues, and the media that might predict variations in the agenda setting effect.

- *Need for Orientation*: Research done by Weaver in 1977 suggested that individuals vary on their need for orientation. Need for orientation is a combination of the individual's interest on the topic and uncertainty about the issue. The higher levels of interest and uncertainty produce higher levels of need for orientation. So the individual would be considerably likely to be influenced by the media stories (psychological aspect of theory) (Miller, 2005).

- *Issue Obtrusiveness*: Research performed by Zucker (1978) suggested that an issue is obtrusive if most members of the public have had direct contact with it, and less obtrusive if audience members have not had direct experience. This means that agenda setting results should be strongest for unobtrusive issues because audience members must rely on media for information on these topics (Miller, 2005).

LEVELS OF AGENDA SETTING

- First-level agenda setting This is the level that is most traditionally studied by researchers. In this level the media use objects or issues to influence the public. In this level the media suggest what the public should think about (amount of coverage).
- Second-level agenda setting. In this level the media focuses on the characteristics of the objects or issues. In this level the media suggest how the people should think about the issue. There are two types of attributes: cognitive (subtantative, or topics) and affective (evaluative, or positive, negative, neutral).
- Intermedia agenda setting (salience transfer among the media) (Coleman and Banning 2006; Lee 2005; Shoemaker & Reese, 1996).

Important Concepts

- *Gatekeeping*--Control over the selection of content discussed in the media; what the public know and care about at any given time is mostly a product of media gatekeeping.
- *Priming*--Effects of particular, prior context on retrieval and interpretation of information. The media's content will provide a lot of time and space

to certain issues, making these issues more accessible and vivid in the public's mind (Miller, 2005).

- *Framing*--Framing is a process of selective control over media content or public communication. Framing defines how a certain piece of media content is packaged so it will influence particular interpretations. This is accomplished through the use of selection, emphasis, exclusion, and elaboration. This is central to second-level agenda setting.

Usage of Theory

- political advertising
- political campaigns and debates
- business news and corporate reputation (Carroll & McCombs, 2003)
- business influence on federal policy (Berger, 2001)
- legal systems, trials (Ramsey & McGuire, 2000)
- role of groups, audience control, public opinion
- public relations (Carroll & McCombs, 2003)

Strengths of Theory

- It has explanatory power because it explains why most people prioritize the same issues as important.
- It has predictive power because it predicts that if people are exposed to the same media, they will feel the same issues are important.
- It can be proven false. If people aren't exposed to the same media, they won't feel the same issues are important.
- Its meta-theoretical assumptions are balanced on the scientific side.
- It lays groundwork for further research.
- It has organizing power because it helps organize existing knowledge of media effects.

Limitations

- Media users may be as ideal as the theory assumes. People may not be well-informed, deeply engaged in public affairs, thoughtful and skeptical. Instead, they pay casual and intermittent attention to public affairs, often ignorant of the details.
- For people who have made up their minds, the effect is weakened.
- News cannot create and conceal problems. The effect can merely alter the awareness, priorities and salience people attached to a set of problems.

Media Influence

In psychology, communication theory and sociology, media influence or media effects refers to the theories about the ways in which the mass media affect how their audiences, think and behave.

The growth of media as an industry has accelerated over the past few years with new forms such as DVD and the internet changing the way we, the audience, consume and receive media. This has caused some media theorists to call into question the influence that the media have over our attitudes and beliefs.

Urbanization, industrialization and modernization have created the societal conditions for the development of mass media. The bulk of the content of the mass media is not designed to challenge or modify the social and political structure of a nation, either in a one party state or in a democratic society. The mass media plays a crucial role in forming and reflecting public opinion: it communicates the world to individuals, and it reproduces modern society's self-image. Critiques in the early-to-mid twentieth century suggested that the media destroys the individual's capacity to act autonomously-sometimes being ascribed an influence reminiscent of the telescreens of the dystopian novel 1984.

Later empirical studies, however, suggest a more complex interaction between the media and society, with individuals actively interpreting and evaluating the media and the information it provides. The consequences and ramifications of the mass media relate not merely to the way newsworthy events are perceived (and which are reported at all), but also to a multitude of cultural influences which operate through the mass media. Thus Lang and Lang claim that "The mass media force attention to certain issues. They build up public images of political figures. They are constantly presenting objects suggesting what individuals in the mass should think about, know about, have feelings about."

Passive Audience Theories

The most common theories of media effects and influence are direct effect or passive audience theories. While not widely held by many academics in the field of communications theory, many of their predictions are assumed by politicians and the public at large.

The hypodermic needle model is a theory that has been held by media theorists since the early 19th century and suggests that the media can be seen as an 'intravenous injection' of message. In other words, any message conveyed by the media is willingly and unquestioningly accepted for its preferred reading by the audience. Certain events support this theory, such as the 1938 radio play of The War of the Worlds by Orson Welles that was broadcast in the United States, its realistic tone and execution inciting panic within the audience and causing riots in towns. However, this theory is discredited by common sense observation. If this theory is nomothetic as it suggests, then we would all respond immediately to any media text we consume. Therefore, the theory's flaw lies in the vast number of intervening variables that alter a person's perception of media messages.

Another example of a passive audience theory is the Inoculation model which is a long term effect model. This states that upon being exposed to a media message, the audience becomes immediately 'immune' to them. So, for example, long term exposure to a violent message will result in a desensitization to that degree of violence. This theory was used to explain the case of James Bulger, in which two boys murdered a child. This invoked a moral panic that saw the film Child's Play 3 being blamed for the violent behaviour. However, there was no evidence that the Inoculation effect had led to this. In fact, there was little to suggest that boys had even seen the film. However, this theory suffers from the same shortfalls as the Hypodermic syringe effect. It sees the audience as entirely passive and impressionable. Therefore, it is commonly discredited by media theorists.

Violence

Media effects theory is the sociological or media studies theory that exposure to representations of violence in any of various media causes (or tends to cause) increased aggression or violence in the audience / consumer. It appears in 'folk wisdom' and newspaper editorials as the claim that x or y media product must be banned in order to avoid the violence it depicts being acted out in society, notably by young people. Some argue that it is not really a theory, as it lacks a meaningful theoretical grounding; instead it is more like a hypothesis.

The most influential studies on the debate around media studies have usually been headline-grabbing 'proofs' of Effects theory. Subsequent attempts to replicate, modify, refine or reject these headline studies have proven of less interest to the mass media.

Examples of Direct Effect Theories on Violence in the Mass Media

Bobo Doll

This classic study (Bandura et al, 1961) exposed two groups of nursery children to a new play area, containing a selection of toys with which they were unfamiliar. One of the toys was a threefoot inflatable Bobo Clown with a weighted base, designed as a self-righting 'punchbag' toy. As they played, the non-aggression (control) set observed an adult playing quietly with certain toys and ignoring Bobo. In the aggression set, the adult 'model' performed a distinctive set of violent moves on Bobo, such as sitting on its head and punching its nose, striking it with a toy mallet, and kicking it into the air, while uttering aggressive phrases such as Punch him in the nose!. Independent observers later scored children's behaviour for aggression when left alone to play with these toys. Those exposed to the 'aggressive' adult demonstrably imitated many of the adult's moves.

Rock 'n Roll

On August 9, 1969 Charles Manson and his cult killed several people, inspired by songs of The Beatles (Piggies, Helter Skelter). This was not the first time a possible negative influence of rock 'n roll was discussed, but it was the first serious case.

In 1980 former Beatle John Lennon was shot. His killer, Mark David Chapman was inspired by Lennon's music and the book The Catcher in the Rye by J.D. Salinger.

In the eighties criticism of rock and especially heavy metal increased. Several cases where fans of metal, gothic or other extreme rock committed murder or suicide were held up by Christian and other pression groups to censor these acts or their music.

In 1985 hearings of this case started and several pop artists came to prevent censorship of the PMRC. It was pointed out that many of these cases were marginal deeds and that the numerous normal fans of this music proved that listening to metal or other sorts of music with controversial topics didn't necessarily end in copycat behaviour. Also by preventing children from hearing this music adult listeners were prevented from hearing these songs and albums too.

One of the most vocal rock musicians to speak out against government censorship in the music industry was Frank Zappa who stated that according to the theories about media influence on people one might say that "everyone who ever listened to The Beatles or The Beach Boys is a potential murderer, because those were the favourite groups of Charles Manson.

Most songs are about love, so if people were really influenced by music: we would all love each other." In the end the Parental Advisory stickers were established.

When Nirvana singer Kurt Cobain committed suicide in 1994 this resulted in several copy cat suicides by fans, which again raised the question if certain rock music should be prevented from release.

Comedian Bill Hicks made a well known conference about rock music influencing suicidal tendencies.

A Clockwork Orange

Stanley Kubrick's film A Clockwork Orange (1971) caused controversy on its release due to the violent content. Alex, the main character, rapes women and beats up beggars. The film tells the story through Alex's eyes and therefore he is represented as a hero while the caricatural people who surround him seem less attractive by comparison. The controversy about the film increased when some gangs and youths started to copycat the violence and rape. The media focused heavily on these cases of copy cat violence and even Kubrick himself started regretting he directed the film. He censored the film in England until after his death (in 1999) to avoid further violence and because of death threats against him and his family.

Cartoon Censorship

In the seventies several classic cartoons were censored when broadcast on television because they were considered a bad influence on children. Some of them because of racist or stereotypical references, but others for their violent content. Especially Looney Tunes and Tom & Jerry were singled out because the cartoons often showcased explosions, gunshots, physical deformations and weapons. Cartoon characters however always survive these actions which, in the eyes of critics, is an unrealistic message to children who might believe when you hurt or kill someone he will remain unharmed.

Many classic cartoons were showed in a censored way where all the violent actions were cut out. Animation fans and the animators themselves criticized this censorship because the pictures became increasingly short and dull, due to the missing of many funny gags.

They pointed out that since the 1940s nearly everyone in the country had grown up watching these cartoons without any negative effects while growing up. Also, the censorship didn't consider the entertainment value of the cartoons.

In the early '90s a boy was assumed to have set fire to his little sisters' bed because he saw a similar scene in an episode of Beavis & Butthead. Controversy arose, but it turned out the boy didn't have cable. MTV did however schedule the program on a later hour.

The Simpsons episode "Itchy and Scratchy and Marge" satirized the censorship of violent cartoons. Itchy & Scratchy themselves are a parody of violence in child oriented media and it's influence on children.

John Hinckley Jr.

In 1981 president Ronald Reagan was shot by John Hinckley Jr.. The president survived and Hinckley was arrested. Just like Lennon's killer Mark David Chapman he had J.D. Salinger's The Catcher in the Rye with him. Hinckley claimed to have committed his crime to impress actress Jodie Foster, like he had seen in the movie Taxi Driver by Martin Scorsese.

The Hungerford Massacre

On August 19, 1987 the British village of Hungerford fell victim to a man, dressed as Rambo, who shot 16 people and wounded 15 others. Afterwards he committed suicide. Although later investigations concluded that he had never seen the film, he did have a collection of other violent movies, which may have inspired the killings.

The Jamie Bulger Case

There has been a long running argument as to whether or not films have influenced people to head out and commit acts of violence and murder. One of the major front runners in this issue is the Jamie Bulger story. On February 12, 1993 in Merseyside, Robert Thompson and Jon Venables (both aged 10) kidnapped, abused and murdered the young toddler Jamie Bulger. The two boys were arrested and instantly the story gained mass media coverage, soon after, it was alleged that the two boys had recently seen the film Child's Play 3, the media instantly took hold of this and the film was seen as the cause of the murder of Jamie Bulger. During the trial, the judge suggested that the film was to blame for the two boys' actions. The media scare at this time was used by UK Prime Minister John Major as propaganda to try to steer children away from glue sniffing and mischief.

The BBC called it a "landmark case" as it was a moral panic about children the threat of other's, and the defenselessness of our own. After the image of a small figure being taken away by two slightly larger figures was all over the tabloids, sales of toddler reins shot up, and in a survey of parents by the children's organization, Kidscape, 97% of respondents put abduction as their biggest worry, ahead of traffic accidents, glue-sniffing and AIDS.

The Columbine Killings

In 1999 two boys shot several students to death in Columbine High School in Colorado. Afterwards they committed suicide. Accusations were made that they were influenced by violent videogames and/or films or goth music. (See Columbine High School Massacre)

In Michael Moore's documentary about these killings, Bowling for Columbine (2002), he examines the possible inspirations for these horrible deeds. He interviews two persons who are frequently criticized for their supposed negative influence on society: rock musician Marilyn Manson and Matt Stone of South Park. Moore comes to the conclusion that these and other media influences do not necessarily lead to copycat cases. He states that the two murderers committed the massacre while the Kosovo War was occurring and that they went bowling before the massacre. The war in Kosovo was a real deed of violence, but virtually no one accused Bill Clinton or the US military of inspiring the murders. If television programs, computer games and rock music are considered possible inspirations why couldn't bowling be the cause? This ridiculous claim shows Moore's point. If you can connect the massacre to rock being listened to days ago, why can't you connect bowling played directly beforehand? This is a classic case of correlation vs. causation.

It is shown that guns are relatively easy to buy in stores and American news broadcasts tend to be so sensational and often scaring in their delivery of events that mass hysteria erupts. People get so frightened and/or disturbed that they overreact to certain things and feel so unsafe they want to buy weapons for protection.

Congressional Hearings, 1981

These hearings were called in response to rising awareness of crime, and the widespread belief that television was at least partly responsible. The National Institute of Mental Health argued forcefully that a broad review of the then-existing literature confirmed Effects theory. Other organizations, eg CBS, submitted contrary position papers-CBS's was entitled "Research on Television Violence: The Fact of Dissent"

Memory

Media can also influence the way people talk. Certain movies have quotes that can be embedded into the minds of the audience. However, these quotes can be either appropriate or nonappropriate. Most of the time they tend to fall into the nonappropriate section.

In justice

- Many famous trials about celebrities such as Roscoe Fatty Arbuckle and Michael Jackson have, whatever the outcome of the trials, ended in such bad publicity and negative depictions of the people involved that their reputation was damaged sincerely forever. The general public had already formed their opinion even before the trials were held. Even if the celebrity remained out of jail or was proven not guilty his career or popularity could have turned out for the worse due to this.

In Politics

- Joseph McCarthy's hunt for communist infiltrations in the US was broadcast frequently on television and other media. Therefore influencing the negative attitude of Americans towards communism, without a neutral viewpoint.
- The election of many politicians since the 1960s, most notably John F. Kennedy in the US have been influenced enormously by media exposure, such as television. Kennedy's victory in the presidential race of 1960 against Richard Nixon has been described as the result of his more handsome and good looking appearance on television, especially when compared with Nixon.

Also Ronald Reagan and Arnold Schwarzenegger whose fame as actors helped them to gain more media attention and eventually the victory in their elections as governor or president. This trend however, can be seen internationally.

In Music

- On August 9, 1969 Charles Manson and his cult killed several people, inspired by songs of The Beatles (Piggies, Helter Skelter). This was not the first time the negative influence of rock 'n roll was discussed, but it was the first serious case.
- In 1980 former Beatle John Lennon was shot. His killer, Mark David Chapman was inspired by Lennon's music and the book The Catcher in the Rye by J.D. Salinger.
- In the eighties criticism of rock and especially heavy metal increased. Several cases where fans of metal, gothic or other extreme rock committed murder or suicide were held up by Christian and other pressure groups to censor these acts or their music.

In 1985 hearings of this case started and several pop artists came to speak against the censorship efforts of the PMRC. It was pointed out that many of these cases were marginal deeds and that the numerous normal fans of this music proved that listening to metal or other sorts of music with controversial topics didn't necessarily lead to copycat behaviour. Also, preventing children from hearing this music adult listeners were prevented of hearing these songs and albums as well.

One of the rock musicians who spoke against government censorship in the music industry was Frank Zappa who stated that, according to the theories about media influence on people, one might say that "everyone who ever listened to The Beatles or The Beach Boys is a potential murderer, because those were the favourite groups of Charles Manson. Most songs are about love, so if people were really influenced by music: we would all love each other." In the end the Parental Advisory stickers were established.

- When Nirvana singer Kurt Cobain committed suicide in 1994 this resulted in several copy cat suicides by fans, which again raised the question if certain rock music should be prevented from release.

In Film

- Stanley Kubrick's film A Clockwork Orange (1971) caused controversy on its release due to the violent content of fights, rape and murder which are presented through the eyes of the gangs who commit them. The controversy about the film increased when some gangs and youths started to copycat the violence and rape. Kubrick then withdrew the film from syndication in England until his death.

"A Clockwork Orange" tells the story of how Alex is cured of his violent behaviour by aversion therapy. Alex is given a nausea inducing drug and is then forced to watch video footage of violent behaviours. After successive pairings Alex becomes physically ill when presented with such stimuli and so avoids these behaviours altogether.

- In 1981 president Ronald Reagan was shot by John Hinckley Jr.. The president survived and Hinckley was arrested. Just like Lennon's killer, Mark David Chapman, he had a copy of J.D. Salinger's "The Catcher in the Rye" with him. Hinckley claimed to have committed his crime to impress actress Jodie Foster, whom he had seen in the movie Taxi Driver by Martin Scorsese.
- On August 19, 1987 a man who dressed himself up as Rambo shot 16 people and wounded 15 others in the British village Hungerford. Afterwards he committed suicide. Although later investigations concluded that he had never seen the film, he did have a collection of other violent movies, which may have inspired him in the killings.

Primary, Secondary and Tertiary Involvement

It has been suggested that the extent to which an audience engages with a media text can be roughly split into three degrees. The first of these is primary involvement, in which the audience is solely concentrating on consuming the media text. For example, they are sitting down solely to watch their favourite program on television. Secondary involvement is when an audience's concentration is split between the media text and another distraction. For example, working on the computer while watching television. Tertiary involvement is when the media text is merely in the background, with no real concentration upon it at all. For example, glancing at a newspaper on a crowded train. While this theory is somewhat simplistic, it provides a clear and probable explanation as to the changes in audience reception.

Perhaps the most widely accepted theory on audience reception is Denis McQuail's Uses and Gratifications model. This places emphasis on why audiences consume media. The first reason outlined in the model are the need to reinforce your own behaviour by identifying with roles and values presented in the media. Secondly, we need to feel some kind of interaction with other people; this is offered by text such as soap operas and lifestyle magazines. The third reason is the need for security in our lifes. Media offer us a window to the world that allows education and the acquisition of information. The final reason is the need for entertainment through both escapism and the need for emotional release, such as laughter. A strength of this theory is the emphasis on the audience as active in the reception of media. However, this would suggest no passivity within the audience whatsoever. A person may, for example, be too lazy to turn off their television and so consume any media that is available. This theory also pays little attention to the short term and long term effects of media on the audience.

Criticism: Criticism of effects theory takes three broad strands.

- Methodological criticisms focus on hidden assumptions, flawed experimental design, and prejudicial interpretation of results of studies claimed to support effects theory.
- Historical criticisms situate the 'meta-narrative' of effects theory within a long history of distrust of new forms of media, dating as far back as Socrates's objections to the deleterious effects due to the written alphabet.
- Political criticisms pose an alternative conception of humans as rational, critical subjects, who are alert to genre norms and adept at interpreting and critiquing media representations, not passively absorbing them.

Supporters of effects theory contend that commercials, advertising and voter campaigns prove that the media influences people's behaviour. In the 20th century aggressive media attention and negative depictions of trials revolving around celebrities as Roscoe Fatty Arbuckle or Michael Jackson have influenced the general public's opinion, before the trials effectively started. However, these critics do point out that while the media could have an effect on people's behaviour this isn't necessarily always the case.

Critics of the media effects theory point out that many copycat murders, suicides and other violent acts nearly always happen in abnormal upbringings. They were raised in a violent, emotionally neglected or aggressive environment which influenced their behaviour more rather than watching certain programs, films or listening to certain music. Most people who carry out these acts are also mentally unstable to begin with.

Critics also point out that just because an audience sees acts of violence on TV, etc, this does not mean they will actually do it themselves. Of the millions of people who watch violent films, only a small number have carried out acts of violence as a direct result. People regularly exposed to violent media usually grow up to be completely normal people. If there are any effects from media, they only affect a very small amount of people.

Political

Certain groups tend to argue for media effects in an effort to promote a political cause. Demands for the banning of certain songs or the labelling of obscene albums came specifically from conservative political groups in the United States. They argued-without evidence-that such material had simple and identifiable effects on children, and this should be banned/labelled.

Priming and Framing

The agenda setting process is partly one which is an almost unavoidable function of the process involved in newsgathering by the large organisations which make up much of the mass media. (Just four main news agencies-AP, UPI, Reuters and Agence-France-Presse-claim together to provide 90% of the total news output of the world's press, radio and television.) Stuart Hall points out that because some of the media produce material which often is good, impartial, and serious, they are accorded a high degree of respect and authority. But in practice the ethic of the press and television is closely related to that of the homogeneous establishment, providing a vital support for the existing order. But independence (eg of the BBC) is not "a mere cover, it is central to the way power and ideology are mediated in societies like ours." The public are bribed with good radio, television and newspapers into an acceptance of the biased, the misleading, and the status quo. The media are not, according to this approach, crude agents of propaganda. They organise public understanding. However, the overall interpretations they provide in the long run are those which are most preferred by, and least challenging to, those with economic power. Greg Philo demonstrates this in his 1991 article, "Seeing is Believing", in which he showed that recollections of the 1984 miners' strike were strongly correlated with the media's original presentation of the event, including the perception of the picketing as largely violent (violence was rare), and the use of phrases which had appeared originally in the media of the time.

McCombs and Shaw (1972) demonstrate the agenda-setting effect at work in a study conducted in Chapel Hill, North Carolina, USA during the 1968 presidential elections. Having selected a representative sample of un-decided voters, they were asked to outline the key issues of the election as they perceived them. Concurrently, the mass media serving these subjects were collected and analysed as regards their content. The results showed a definite correlation between the two accounts of predominant issues. "The evidence in this study that voters tend to share the media's composite definition of what is important strongly suggests an agenda-setting function of the mass media." (McCombs and Shaw).

New Media

Theorists such as Louis Wirth and Talcott Parsons have emphasised the importance of mass media as instruments of social control. In the twenty-first century, with the rise of the internet, the two-way relationship between mass media and public opinion is beginning to change, with the advent of new technologies such as blogging.

Mander's theory is related to Jean Baudrillard's concept of 'hyperreality'. We can take the 1994 O.J. Simpson trial as an example, where the reality reported on was merely the catalyst for the simulacra (images) created, which defined the trial as a global event and made the trial more than it was. Essentially, hyperreality is the concept that the media is not merely a window on to the world (as if a visiting alien were watching TV), but is itself part of the reality it describes. Hence (although additionally there is the question of navel-gazing) the media's obsession with media-created events. It is this which lead Marshall McLuhan in the 1960s to say that "the medium is the message", and to suggest that mass media was increasingly creating a "global village". Thus, for example, there is evidence that Western media influences in Asia are the driving force behind rapid social change: "it is as if the 1960s and the 1990s were compressed together." A notable example is the recent introduction of television to Bhutan, with dramatic effects in terms of very rapid Westernization. This raises questions of 'cultural imperialism' (Schiller)-the de facto imposition, through economic and political power and through the media, of Western (and in particular US) culture.

An Instrument for Social Control

Social scientists have made efforts to integrate the study of the mass media as instrument of control with the study of political and economic developments in the Afro-Asian countries. David Lerner(1958) has emphasised the general pattern of increase in standard of living, urbanization, literacy and exposer to the mass media during the process of transition from traditional to modern society. According to Lerner, while there is a heavy emphasis on the expanding of the mass media in developing societies, the penetration of the central authority into the daily consciousness of the mass has to overcome profound resistance.

6

Government and Mass Media

INTRODUCTION

The commission on Freedom of the press (1947) has listed most political and legal controls that have commonly been applied to the media. They include licensing in advance; censorship of offending material before publication; seizure of offending material; injunctions against publication of a newspaper or book or of specified content; requirement of surety bonds against libel or other offense; compulsory disclosure of ownership and authority; post publication criminal penalties for objectionable matter; post publication collection of damages in a civil action; post publication correction of libel and other misstatements; discrimination in granting access to news source and facilities; discrimination and denial in the use of communications facilities for distribution; taxes; discriminatory subsidies; and interference with buying, reading and listening.

THE PUBLIC SPHERE

Structural Transformation

Habermas believed that society becomes increasingly polarised into spheres of "public authority"-referring to the emergence of the state and associated political activity-and the "private"-the intimate domain of private relationships and the family. Jürgen Habermas believed that the development of mass media was a crucial factor in the transition from an absolutist regime to liberal-democratic society. With the invention of the printing press and then the availability of newspapers and other forms of printed literature, Habermas claimed the emergence of an intermediate sphere which according to him is the bourgeois public sphere. This space will provide individuals with a chance to gather together to critically access, discuss and evaluate important contemporary issues of utmost importance for the people. He claimed that this will resemble the Greek agora. Habermas claims that this public use of reason not only acts as a regulatory mechanism over the state, which is now highly visible, but also as a catalyst for the replacement of the absolutist regime with a liberal democratic government.

Frankfurt School

The Frankfurt School came into existence in order to explain the success of Nazism in Weimar Germany. It sees the loss of individuality through decline of privacy as the main cause of dependence on great mass organisations. Habermas to a certain extent depends on some early critiques of the media from the 'Frankfurt School', such as that of Max Horkheimer, Theodor Adorno and Herbert Marcuse. For these three, media was a 'culture industry' which was creating an impact on passive individuals. These individuals merely absorb any information they are exposed to. (A clear influence of Karl Marx can be seen here, with links to the theory of alienation.) According to Thompson, the cause of this is the commodification of art and culture, which allows the possibility of "manipulation by demagogues". Emile Durkheim claimed that the interdependence of highly specialised individuals, or what is known as 'organic solidarity', is seen as being succeeded by a new and barbarous homogeneity. Due to this, only a 'mechanical' cohesion is possible, dependent on similarity and standardisation. Horkheimer thus argued that, paradoxically, individuality was impaired by the decline in the impulse for collective action. According to him, 'As the ordinary man withdraws from participating in political affairs, society tends to revert to the law of the jungle, which crushes all vestiges of individuality.' In this analysis the Frankfurt school saw totalitarianism emerging as a result of corrupt social institutions and the decline of liberal principles. Thus Horkheimer claimed that: "Just as the slogans of rugged individualism are politically useful to large trusts in society seeking exemption from social control, so in mass culture the rhetoric of individuality, by imposing patterns for collective imitation, subverts the very principle to which it gives lip service." Adorno in The Jargon of Authenticity claimed that "mass media can create an aura which makes the spectator seem to experience a non-existent actuality". Thus a mass-produced, artificial culture replaces what went before.

Mass Media and Modern Public Sphere

In political behaviour, opinion leading tends to correlate positively with status, whereas this is not the case in consumer behaviour. So for political behaviour, the general conclusion that the media merely fixes (confirms) people's opinion is not supported. Hovland, using experimental psychology, found significant effects of information on longer-term behaviour and attitudes, particularly in areas where most people have little direct experience (e.g. politics) and have a high degree of trust in the source (e.g. broadcasting). Since class has become a less reliable indicator of party (since the surveys of the 40s and 50s) the floating voter today is no longer the apathetic voter, but likely to be more well-informed than the consistent voter-and this mainly through the media.

There is also some very persuasive and empirical evidence suggesting that it is 'personal contact, not media persuasiveness' which counts. For example, Trenaman and McQuail (1961) found that 'don't knows' were less well informed than consistent voters, appearing uninterested, showing a general lack of information, and not just ignorance of particular policies or policies of one particular party. During the 1940 presidential election, a similar view was expressed by Katz and Lazarsfeld's theory of the two-step flow of communication, based on a study of electoral practices of the citizens of Erie County, Ohio. This examined the political propaganda prevalent in the media at the time during the campaign period to see whether it plays an integral role in influencing people's voting. (In terms of generalising their results, one should note that there are questions about short term versus long term influence). The results contradict this: Lazarsfeld et al (1944) find evidence for the Weberian theory of party, and identify certain factors, such as socio-economic circumstances, religious affiliation and area of residence, which together determine political orientation. The study claims that political propaganda serves to re-affirm the individual's pre-disposed orientation rather than to influence or change one's voting behaviour.

Thompson does not see 'mediated quasi-interaction' (the monological, mainly one-way communication of the mass media) as dominant, but rather as intermingling with traditional face-to-face interactions and mediated interactions (such as telephone conversations). Contrary to Habermas' pessimistic view, this allows both more information and discussion to come into the public domain (of mediated quasi-interaction) and more to be discussed within the private domain (since the media provides information individuals would not otherwise have access to).

MASS MEDIA IN A FREE ENTERPRISE SOCIETY

Although a sizeable portion of mass media offerings-particularly news, commentaries, documentaries, and other informational programmes-deal with highly controversial subjects, the major portion of mass media offerings are designed to serve an entertainment function. These programmes tend to avoid controversial issues and reflect beliefs and values sanctified by mass audience. This course is followed by Television networks, whose investment and production costs are high. Jerry Mander's work has highlighted this particular outlook. According to him, the atomised individuals of mass society lose their souls to the phantom delights of the film, the soap opera, and the variety show. They fall into a stupor; an apathetic hypnosis Lazarsfeld was to call the 'narcotizing dysfunction' of exposure to mass media. Individuals become 'irrational victims of false wants'- the wants which corporations have thrust upon them, and continue to thrust upon them, through both the advertising in the media (with its continual exhortation to consume) and through the individualist consumption culture it promulgates. Thus, according to the Frankfurt School, leisure has been industrialised. The production of culture had become standardised and dominated by the profit motive as in other industries. In a mass society leisure is constantly used to induce the appropriate values and motives in the public. The modern media train the young for consumption. 'Leisure had ceased to be the opposite of work, and had become a preparation for it.'

Mass Media, Mass Culture and Elite

The relation of the mass media to contemporary popular culture is commonly conceived in terms of dissemination from the elite to the mass. There are periods when this process is reversed. During the 18th century it was the utmost chic for the aristocrats of the French Court to assume the guise of shepherds and peasants in their restive outings.

The long-term consequences of this are significant in conjunction with the continuing concentration of ownership and control of the media, leading to accusations of a 'media elite' having a form of 'cultural dictatorship'. Thus the continuing debate about the influence of 'media barons' such as Conrad Black and Rupert Murdoch. For example, the UK Observer (March 1st 1998) reported the Murdoch-owned HarperCollins' refusal to publish Chris Patten's East and West, because of the former Hong Kong Governor's description of the Chinese leadership as "faceless Stalinists" possibly being damaging to Murdoch's Chinese broadcasting interests. In this case, the author was able to have the book accepted by another publisher, but this kind of censorship may point the way to the future. A related, but more insidious, form is that of self-censorship by members of the media in the interests of the owner, in the interests of their careers.

COMMUNICATION THEORY

There is much discussion in the academic world of communication as to what actually constitutes communication. Currently, many definitions of communication are used in order to conceptualize the processes by which people navigate and assign meaning.

We might say that communication consists of transmitting information from one person to another. In fact, many scholars of communication take this as a working definition, and use Lasswell's maxim, "who says what to whom in what channel with what effect," as a means of circumscribing the field of communication theory.

Other commentators suggest that a ritual process of communication exists, one not artificially divorceable from a particular historical and social context.

Communication stands so deeply rooted in human behaviours and the structures of society that scholars have difficulty thinking of it while excluding social or behavioural events. Because communication theory remains a relatively young field of inquiry and integrates itself with other disciplines such as philosophy, psychology, and sociology, one probably cannot yet expect a consensus conceptualization of communication across disciplines.

Currently, there is no paradigm from which communication scholars may work. One of the issues facing scholars is the possibility that establishing a communication metatheory will negate their research and stifle the broad body of knowledge in which communication functions.

History

In the history of philosophy, Aristotle first addressed the problem of communication and attempted to work out a theory of it in The Rhetoric. He was primarily focused on the art of persuasion.

Humanistic and rhetorical viewpoints and theories dominated the discipline prior to the twentieth century, when more scientific methodologies and insights from psychology, sociology, linguistics and advertising began to influence communication thought and practice.

Framework

It is helpful to examine communication and communication theory through one of the following viewpoints:

- *Mechanistic:* This view considers communication to be a perfect transaction of a message from the sender to the receiver. (as seen in the diagram above)
- *Psychological:* This view considers communication as the act of sending a message to a receiver, and the feelings and thoughts of the receiver upon interpreting the message.
- *Social Constructionist (Symbolic Interactionist):* This view considers communication to be the product of the interactants sharing and creating meaning.
- *Systemic:* This view considers communication to be the new messages created via "through-out", or what happens as the message is being interpreted and re-interpreted as it travels through people.

Inspection of a particular theory on this level will provide a framework on the nature of communication as seen within the confines of that theory.

Theories can also be studied and organized according to the ontological, epistemological, and axiological framework imposed by the theorist. Ontology essentially poses the question of what, exactly, it is the theorist is examining. One must consider the very nature of reality. The answer usually falls in one of three realms depending on whether the theorist sees the phenomena through the lens of a realist, nominaist, or social constructionist. Realist perspective view the world objectively, believing that there is a world outside of our own experience and cognitions. Nominalists see the world subjectively, claiming that everything outside of one's cognitions is simply names and labels. Social constructionists straddle the fence between objective and subjective reality, claiming that reality is what we create together.

Epistemology is an examination of how the theorist studies the chosen phenomena. In studying epistemology, objective knowledge is said to be the result of a systematic look at the causal relationships of phenomena. This knowledge is usually attained through use of the scientific method. Scholars often think that empirical evidence collected in an objective manner is most likely to reflect truth in the findings. Theories of this ilk are usually created to predict a phenomenon. Subjective theory holds that understanding is based on situated knowledge, typically found using interpretative methodology such as ethnography and interviews. Subjective theories are typically developed to explain or understand phenomena in the social world.

Axiology is concerned with what values drive a theorist to develop a theory. Theorists must be mindful of potential biases so that they will not influence or skew their findings (Miller, 21-23).

MAPPING THE THEORETICAL LANDSCAPE

A discipline gets defined in large part by its theoretical structure. Communication studies often borrow theories from other social sciences. This theoretical variation makes it difficult to come to terms with the field as a whole. That said, some common taxonomies exist that serve to divide up the range of communication research. Two common mappings involve contexts and assumptions.

Contexts

Many authors and researchers divide communication by what they sometimes called "contexts" or "levels", but which more often represent institutional histories. The study of communication in the US, while occurring within departments of psychology, sociology, linguistics, and anthropology (among others), generally developed from schools of rhetoric and from schools of journalism. While many of these have become "departments of communication", they often retain their historical roots, adhering largely to theories from speech communication in the former case, and from mass media in the latter. The great divide between speech communication and mass communication becomes complicated by a number of smaller sub-areas of communication research, including intercultural and international communication, small group communication, communication technology, policy and legal studies of communication, telecommunication, and work done under a variety of other labels. Some of these departments take a largely social-scientific perspective, others tend more heavily toward the humanities, and still others gear themselves more toward production and professional preparation.

These "levels" of communication provide some way of grouping communication theories, but inevitably, some theories and concepts leak from one area to another, or fail to find a home at all.

Assumptions

Another way of dividing up the communication field emphasizes the assumptions that undergird particular theories, models, and approaches. While this approach also tends to have as its basis institutional divisions, theories within each of the seven "traditions" of communication theory that Robert Craig suggests tend to reinforce one another, and retain the same ground epistemological and axiological assumptions. His traditions include:

- rhetorical-practical art of discourse
- semiotic-intersubjective mediation through signs
- phenomenological-experience of otherness, dialogue
- cybernetic-information processing
- sociopsychological-expression, interaction and influence
- critical-discursive reflection
- sociocultural-reproduction of social order (Miller, 13)

Craig finds each of these clearly defined against the others, and remaining cohesive approaches to describing communicative behaviour. As a taxonomic aid, these labels help to organize theory by its assumptions, and help researchers to understand why some theories may seem incommensurable.

While communication theorists very commonly use these two approaches, it seems that they decentralize the place of language and machines as communicative technologies. The idea (as argued by Vygotsky) of communication as the primary tool of a species defined by its tools remains on the outskirts of communication theory.

It finds some representation in the Toronto School of communication theory (alternatively sometimes called medium theory) as represented by the work of Innis, McLuhan, and others. It seems that the ways in which individuals and groups use the technologies of communication-and in some cases are used by them-remain central to what communication researchers do.

The ideas that surround this, and in particular the place of persuasion, remain constants across both the "traditions" and "levels" of communication theory.

Uses and Gratifications

Uses and gratifications, also known as usage and gratifications or needs and gratifications, is not a single approach but a body of approaches to media analysis that developed out of many varied empirical studies, beginning in the mid 20th century.

The basic theme of uses and gratifications is the idea that people use the media to get specific gratifications.

The basic tenet of Uses and Gratifications (called UG for short) is that people are not helpless victims of all powerful media, but use media to fulfil their various needs. These needs serve as motivations (gratifications sought) for using media. Gratifications obtained should correspond with gratifications sought for the media to be able to meet the needs of the users.

Jay G. Blumler and Elihu Katz devised their uses and gratifications model in 1974 to highlight four areas of gratification in media texts for audiences. These include:

1. *Diversion*-a media text which provides escapism. When a media text temporarily partially covers one's senses. For example playing a video game.
2. *Personal Relationships*-People create personal relationships with the characters in a media text, they start to feel they know them. This can become dangerous if people start to trust them as well, for example if one trusted a news reporter too much they may take everything they say at face value and not question it, this trust could then be abused.
3. *Personal Identity*-When a person creates part of their own identity from things they find attractive in people from media texts, for example someone may have a haircut because they liked the look of a similar one in a magazine. This can go a long way in shaping people and people's ideas of values, norms, ideologies and fashions.

4. *Surveillance*-the audience gain an understanding of the world around them by consuming a media text, for example print and broadcast news.

SYMBOLIC CONVERGENCE THEORY

Symbolic Convergence Theory (SCT) is a general communication theory. SCT explains that meanings, emotions, values, and the motives for action are in the rhetoric that is co-created by people trying to make sense out of a common experience, such as university life. SCT posits that students talk about their shared experiences, like a professor they have had in class. During such discussions, a rhetorical fantasy might chain out about a professor that will bring the teacher into dramatic life acting in a classroom scene, often times in humorous ways. A professor might be called "The Red Pheasant" because he has red hair and bobs his head like a pheasant going down a corn row. Or the professor might be called "The Candy Lady" because she brings treats to class.

SCT is a general communication theory because it explains that such fantasy-chaining by people about a common experience produces a rhetorical vision in all communities. Just as students co-create university dramas, so, too, do marines, police officers, firefighters, and members of any organization. SCT argues that people inherently create their own symbolic reality into a stable rhetorical form that can be studied and understood. SCT calls these stable forms of viewing the world (that evolve through human talk), rhetorical visions. These rhetorical visions contain one of three underlying or under-girding master analogues (Righteous, Social, and Pragmatic).

Rhetorical visions are formed from various fantasies that chain out over important issues in the community. There are heroes, villains, and plot-lines for each competing vision. Righteous heroes strive for excellence. These heroes want to be at the cutting edge of their field. They want things done the right way and they need in-depth knowledge to do so. A Righteous hero says: "If you want something done right, do it yourself" Social heroes stress the importance of human ties. For them, humane acts, loyalty, and trust are important values in forming strong, interpersonal bonds. They believe that networking is an important strategy for getting things done. Social heroes say: "You don't have to know everything about the job. You just have to know how to work with people and share knowledge to accomplish common goals. The Pragmatic hero seeks the most efficient and cost-effective strategy to reach a goal with a minimum of intellectual and emotional involvement. A Pragmatic university student says: "I need a university degree which requires the least effort, the fewest dollars, and the fastest time, to get the best job." In a nutshell, if the three competing heroes were discussing how they would change motor oil, the Righteous one would say: "I'll do it myself;" the Social one would say: "I'm having my trusted auto mechanic do it for me;" and the Pragmatic hero would say: "I'm going to Jiffy Lube because it's quicker and cheaper."

Fantasy types are the work-horse of SCT. New rhetorical fantasies are often created from old, existing ones. For example, if you go on the Internet and Google search "The Perfect Storm," the first seven or so hits are stories about the movie by that name in which three bad weather conditions produced monstrous, 100-foot waves that sunk a fish boat. However, the next score of hits reveal a fantasy type. Economic stories are reported that are called "The Perfect Economic Storm," meaning three bad economic events coincided to produce a disastrous business situation. You could have a "Perfect Storm" semester if three bad academic events occurred simultaneously like a professor from hell, an impossible roommate, and a bad case of the flu during finals week.

During the 1972 U.S. presidential election, people working for then-President Nixon broke into the national Democratic

Headquarters in the Watergate Hotel. They were caught, the President tried to cover it up, but eventually he had to resign. This high drama produced a fantasy type that still exists. The French have had their "Wine-gate," and President Reagan had his "Iran-gate." Put "gate" after anything these days and we know it's a plotline that involves administrative corruption and government cover-up. Sometimes a fantasy type is produced by putting "another" in front of an old drama, as in "another Vietnam," or "another Rodney King" case. When a rhetorical community knows one fantasy, they can quickly chain out a new one by making the first fantasy into a fantasy type.

As noted above, rhetorical visions can vary along a number of different continua. As you saw, two continua (Pure to Mixed Master Analogues, and Satisfied to Dissatisfied) produced 12 different visions. If one were to add three more continua (Egalitarian to Elite, Proselytizing to Secretive, and Flexible to Rigid) then there would be 96 potential dramas. However, in reality, most rhetorical communities have only three to seven at any given time. In fact, some communities only have one rhetorical vision. American history is replete with examples of one-vision religious cults. Jimmy Jones' Temple members committed mass ritualistic suicide in Guyana, The Heaven's Gate sect also committed mass ritualistic suicide in San Diego, and the Branch Davidians, in Waco, Texas, died in a confrontation with the FBI. In these extreme, righteous, rigid dramas, any backsliders are punished for even minor deviations from the orthodox vision.

You have probably not been in such an intense rhetorical vision but SCT predicts that you are most likely in several different rhetorical visions simultaneously. For example, you might be in a Righteous student vision at your university but also in a Pragmatic drama in your part-time job, while at the same time in a Social drama about America's place in world affairs. Furthermore, SCT suggests that over time you might migrate from one master analogue-based vision to another. In your first year of college you could have been caught up in a Righteous vision but by your senior year you might find yourself in a very Pragmatic drama about finishing school and getting a job. Regardless of the longevity of a rhetorical vision, SCT explains that visions go through a five-stage lifecycle.

Stage 1: Creation

The genesis story of "In the beginning was the Word." For the University of St. Thomas, it was Bishop Ireland's dream of a Catholic Diocesan university. For the University of Missouri-Kansas City, it concerned the back room political deals necessary to get the legislative votes to have the State of Missouri bail out the bankrupt, private school, the University of Kansas City. The dominant rhetorical vision of your university started with a rich "genesis" story. Do you know what it is?

Stage 2: Consciousness-Raising

This is the stage where fantasies begin to chain out among a collectivity of people over a common interest. As they co-create a new vision, their lives take on new meaning and emotion and their behaviour changes. New members of existing visions often go through this stage in a formal, prescribed way. "Pledge" classes for fraternities and sororities, "boot" camp for Marine recruits, and "retreats" for novices of religious orders are typical examples. The first week or two of college for new students can have a consciousness-raising effect if the university plans ritualistic events designed to assimilate the students into the university's vision. Can you identify any college rituals in which you participated that heightened your sense of belonging to your school or some sub-group, like the band, a debate team, or a sport?

Stage 3: Consciousness-Sustaining

A mature rhetorical vision seeks stability. New members are brought in, old members are retained. The vision must adapt to changing events and provide rebuttals to competing visions. Often times, rhetorical visions can remain stable for 100 years or longer. State Farm Insurance has maintained a dominant, social vision of "Like A Good Neighbour, State Farm Is There," for almost a century. Can you identify any other 100-year-old rhetorical visions?

Stage 4: Vision-Declining

Situations in a rhetorical community can change so rapidly that the vision cannot adapt successfully. After 100 years of being Illinois' oldest teacher-training college, Illinois State Normal Teacher's College changed its name to Illinois State University in 1964. Today, only ten-percent of 18,000 students are education majors. Starting in 1964, the faculty and students began participating in new rhetorical dramas that would give meaning to their place in higher education. Has your university gone through a similar identity crisis as one rhetorical vision declined and a new one began to emerge?

Stage 5: Vision Implosion

Sometimes rhetorical visions instantly implode in the presence of a major event. At other times, the implosion can take years. The Cold War Rhetorical Vision (1947-1990) was a case of instant No implosion. The Righteous Cold War drama portrayed heroic Americans as being in a struggle against God-less Communism. It was a struggle for the hearts and minds of people on a worldwide stage. In 1990, the drama imploded with the sudden collapse of the Soviet Union. The Upjohn Pharmaceutical Co. lasted for 100 years with the slogan: "Keep The Quality Up." In the space of two years, Upjohn merged with another century-old Swedish company only to see the new merged company purchased and dissolved by a third drug company, Pfizer. In the first case, the Cold War warriors could declare victory and look for a new vision of America's role in the world. In the second example, the loyal Upjohn employees felt stripped of their symbolic identity. Have you ever been in a rhetorical vision when it imploded? For example, maybe your old high school closed or merged with another. Maybe your favourite sport was dropped by the university or your major was eliminated. The felt loss is real in terms of meaning, emotion, and motive for action.

What is the utility of SCT for you? SCT explains the way your view of campus life depends upon the rhetorical vision in which you participate. If you are a Righteous student, you probably see SCT as an important communication theory that you can study. In fact, you might want to conduct your own SCT study on your campus by using this research instrument, plus a questionnaire asking demographic (age, gender, etc.), sociographic (behaviours) and psychographic (attitudes and beliefs) questions. If you are a Social student, you might see SCT as yet another way to understand interpersonal communication and how people come to identify with one another. If you are a Pragmatic student, you will see the utility of SCT in designing marketing and Public Relations campaigns and use the theory to improve your job interviewing skills.

7

Information Theory

Information theory is a discipline in applied mathematics involving the quantification of data with the goal of enabling as much data as possible to be reliably stored on a medium or communicated over a channel. The measure of information, known as information entropy, is usually expressed by the average number of bits needed for storage or communication. For example, if a daily weather description has an entropy of 3 bits, then, over enough days, we can describe daily weather with an average of approximately 3 bits per day.

Applications of fundamental topics of information theory include lossless data compression (e.g. ZIP files), lossy data compression (e.g. MP3s), and channel coding (e.g. for DSL lines). The field is at the crossroads of mathematics, statistics, computer science, physics, neurobiology, and electrical engineering. Its impact has been crucial to success of the Voyager missions to deep space, the invention of the CD, the feasibility of mobile phones, the development of the Internet, the study of linguistics and of human perception, the understanding of black holes, and numerous other fields.

AN OVERVIEW

The main concepts of information theory can be grasped by considering the most widespread means of human communication: language. Two important aspects of a good language are as follows: First, the most common words (e.g., "a," "the," "I") should be shorter than less common words (e.g., "benefit," "generation," "mediocre"), so that sentences will not be too long. Such a tradeoff in word length is analogous to data compression and is the essential aspect of source coding. Second, if part of a sentence is unheard or misheard due to noise-e.g., a passing car-the listener should still be able to glean the meaning of the underlying message. Such robustness is as essential for an electronic communication system as it is for a language; properly building such robustness into communications is done by channel coding. Source coding and channel coding are the fundamental concerns of information theory.

Note that these concerns have nothing to do with the importance of messages. For example, a platitude such as "Thank you; come again" takes about as long to say or write as the urgent plea, "Call an ambulance!" while clearly the latter is more important and more meaningful. Information theory, however, does not involve message importance or meaning, as these are matters of the quality of data rather than the quantity of data, the latter of which is determined solely by probabilities.

Information theory is generally considered to have been founded in 1948 by Claude Shannon in his seminal work, "A Mathematical Theory of Communication." The central paradigm of classical information theory is the engineering problem of the transmission of information over a noisy channel. The most fundamental results of this theory are Shannon's source coding theorem, which establishes that, on average, the number of bits needed to represent the result of an uncertain event is given by its entropy; and Shannon's noisy-channel coding theorem, which states that reliable communication is possible over noisy channels provided that the rate of communication is below a certain threshold called the channel capacity. The channel capacity can be approached by using appropriate encoding and decoding systems.

Information theory is closely associated with a collection of pure and applied disciplines that have been investigated and reduced to engineering practice under a variety of rubrics throughout the world over the past half century or more: adaptive systems, anticipatory systems, artificial intelligence, complex systems, complexity science, cybernetics, informatics, machine learning, along with systems sciences of many descriptions. Information theory is a broad and deep mathematical theory, with equally broad and deep applications, amongst which is the vital field of coding theory.

Coding theory is concerned with finding explicit methods, called codes, of increasing the efficiency and reducing the net error rate of data communication over a noisy channel to near the limit that Shannon proved is the maximum possible for that channel. These codes can be roughly subdivided into data compression (source coding) and error-correction (channel coding) techniques. In the latter case, it took many years to find the methods Shannon's work proved were possible. A third class of information theory codes are cryptographic algorithms (both codes and ciphers). Concepts, methods and results from coding theory and information theory are widely used in cryptography and cryptanalysis. See the article ban (information) for a historical application.

Information theory is also used in information retrieval, intelligence gathering, gambling, statistics, and even in musical composition.

HISTORICAL BACKGROUND

The landmark event that established the discipline of information theory, and brought it to immediate worldwide attention, was the publication of Claude E. Shannon's classic paper "A Mathematical Theory of Communication" in the Bell System Technical Journal in July and October of 1948.

Prior to this paper, limited information theoretic ideas had been developed at Bell Labs, all implicitly assuming events of equal probability. Harry Nyquist's 1924 paper, Certain Factors Affecting Telegraph Speed, contains a theoretical section quantifying "intelligence" and the "line speed" at which it can be transmitted by a communication system, giving the relation W = Klogm, where W is the speed of transmission of intelligence, m is the number of different voltage levels to choose from at each time step, and K is a constant. Ralph Hartley's 1928 paper, Transmission of Information, uses the word information as a measurable quantity, reflecting the receiver's ability to distinguish that one sequence of symbols from any other, thus quantifying information as H = logSn = nlogS, where S was the number of possible symbols, and n the number of symbols in a transmission. The natural unit of information was therefore the decimal digit, much later renamed the hartley in his honour as a unit or scale or measure of information. Alan Turing in 1940 used similar ideas as part of the statistical analysis of the breaking of the German second world war Enigma ciphers.

Much of the mathematics behind information theory with events of different probabilities was developed for the field of thermodynamics by Ludwig Boltzmann and J. Willard Gibbs. Connections between information-theoretic entropy and thermodynamic entropy, including the important contributions by Rolf Landauer in the 1960s, are explored in Entropy in thermodynamics and information theory.

In Shannon's revolutionary and groundbreaking paper, the work for which had been substantially completed at Bell Labs by the end of 1944, Shannon for the first time introduced the qualitative and quantitative model of communication as a statistical process underlying information theory, opening with the assertion that

"The fundamental problem of communication is that of reproducing at one point, either exactly or approximately, a message selected at another point."

With it came the ideas of:

- the information entropy and redundancy of a source, and its relevance through the source coding theorem;

- the mutual information, and the channel capacity of a noisy channel, including the promise of perfect loss-free communication given by the noisy-channel coding theorem;
- the practical result of the Shannon-Hartley law for the channel capacity of a Gaussian channel; and of course
- the bit-a new way of seeing the most fundamental unit of information

SPIN (PUBLIC RELATIONS)

In public relations, spin is a usually pejorative term signifying a heavily biased portrayal in one's own favour of an event or situation. While traditional public relations may also rely on creative presentation of the facts, "spin" often, though not always, implies disingenuous, deceptive and/or highly manipulative tactics. Politicians are often accused of spin by their political opponents.

The term is borrowed from ball sports such as cricket, where a spin bowler may impart spin on the ball during a delivery so that it will curve through the air or bounce in an advantageous manner.

Because of the frequent association between "spin" and press conferences (especially government press conferences), the room in which these take place is sometimes described as a spin room. A group of people who develop spin may be referred to as "spin doctors" who engage in "spin doctoring" for the person or group that hired them.

Overview: The techniques of spin include:

- Selectively presenting facts and quotes that support one's position (cherry picking)
- Non-denial denial
- Phrasing in a way that assumes unproven truths
- Euphemisms to disguise or promote one's agenda

PUBLIC AND MEDIA RELATIONS

Before you learn more about public and media relations, you should get a basic impression of what they are. See What's "Advertising, Marketing, Promotion, Public Relations and Publicity, and Sales?".

Public relations includes ongoing activities to ensure the organization has a strong public image. Public relations activities include helping the public to understand the organization and its products. Similar to effective advertising and promotions, effective public relations often depends on designing and implementing a well-designed public relations plan.

The plan often includes description of what you want to convey to whom, how you plan to convey it, who is responsible for various activities and by when, and how much money is budgeted to fund these activities. Similar to advertising and promotions, a media plan and calendar can be very useful, which specifies what media methods that are used and when.

Often, public relations are conducted through the media, that is, newspapers, television, magazines, etc. Publicity is mention in the media. Organizations usually have little control over the message in the media, at least, not as much as they do in advertising. Regarding publicity, reporters and writers decide what will be said.

Regarding public relations, consider: What groups of stakeholders do we want to appeal to and how? What impressions do you want each of your stakeholder to have? What communications media do they see or prefer the most? Consider advertising, collaborations, annual reports, networking, TV, radio, newsletters, classifieds, displays/signs, posters, word of mouth, direct mail, special events, brochures, neighbourhood newsletters, etc. What media is most practical for you to use in terms of access and affordability? What messages are most appealing to each stakeholder group?

MANAGING YOUR IMAGE

You should care deeply about the image that you portray to major stakeholders of your business, for example, to current and potential customers, employees, investors/funders, suppliers, local and state agencies, etc. The following links are to information that will help you design and carry out an approach to ensuring a strong public image for your company.

BASIC DEFINITIONS

It's easy to become confused about these terms: advertising, marketing, promotion, public relations and publicity, and sales. The terms are often used interchangeably. However, they refer to different--but similar activities. Some basic definitions are provided below. A short example is also provided hopefully to help make the terms more clear to the reader.

Advertising

Advertising is bringing a product (or service) to the attention of potential and current customers. Advertising is focused on one particular product or service. Thus, an advertising plan for one product might be very different than that for another product. Advertising is typically done with signs, brochures, commercials, direct mailings or e-mail messages, personal contact, etc.

Promotion

Promotion keeps the product in the minds of the customer and helps stimulate demand for the product. Promotion involves ongoing advertising and publicity (mention in the press). The ongoing activities of advertising, sales and public relations are often considered aspects of promotions.

Marketing

Marketing is the wide range of activities involved in making sure that you're continuing to meet the needs of your customers and getting value in return. Marketing is usually focused on one product or service. Thus, a marketing plan for one product might be very different than that for another product. Marketing activities include "inbound marketing," such as market research to find out, for example, what groups of potential customers exist, what their needs are, which of those needs you can meet, how you should meet them, etc. Inbound marketing also includes analyzing the competition, positioning your new product or service (finding your market niche), and pricing your products and services. "Outbound marketing" includes promoting a product through continued advertising, promotions, public relations and sales.

Public Relations

Public relations includes ongoing activities to ensure the overall company has a strong public image. Public relations activities include helping the public to understand the company and its products. Often, public relations are conducted through the media, that is, newspapers, television, magazines, etc. As noted above, public relations is often considered as one of the primary activities included in promotions.

Publicity

Publicity is mention in the media. Organizations usually have little control over the message in the media, at least, not as they do in advertising. Regarding publicity, reporters and writers decide what will be said.

Sales

Sales involves most or many of the following activities, including cultivating prospective buyers (or leads) in a market segment; conveying the features, advantages and benefits of a product or service to the lead; and closing the sale (or coming to agreement on pricing and services). A sales plan for one product might be very different than that for another product.

Example of the Definitions

The following example may help to make the above five concepts more clear. I recently read that the story comes from the Reader's Digest, a quote found in "Promoting Issues and Ideas" by M. Booth and Associates, Inc. (Thanks to Jennifer M. Seher, participant in the CONSULTANTS@CHARITYCHANNEL.COM on-line discussion group.)

"... if the circus is coming to town and you paint a sign saying 'Circus Coming to the Fairground Saturday', that's advertising. If you put the sign on the back of an elephant and walk it into town, that's promotion. If the elephant walks through the mayor's flower bed, that's publicity. And if you get the mayor to laugh about it, that's public relations." If the town's citizens go the circus, you show them the many entertainment booths, explain how much fun they'll have spending money at the booths, answer their questions and ultimately, they spend a lot at the circus, that's sales.

Major Methods of Advertising and Promotion (Methods of External Communications)

First, A Word About Writing Ads

It's almost useless to review lists of alternatives for advertising if you haven't developed well-written ads. Writing ads is a skill. There are important aspects to think about, including the wording, graphics, arrangement of wording and graphics, coloring, how your audience will interpret the ads, their placement, etc. Poorly done ads can hurt you worse than not having ads at all. Therefore, very carefully consider getting help to write your first ads. (See Writing Your Ad.)

What Should You Write in Your Ads?

The answer to this question depends almost entirely on the reading and listening habits of your current and potential customers. This is where some basic market research can help you a great deal. A lot can be learned by using a few basic methods. (See Basic Methods to Get Customer Feedback and Some Major Sources of Market Research Information.)

Before you write your ads, you should give careful thought to your unique selling position so you know what unique features and benefits to convey and to whom. Review information in Positioning.

Note that a common mistake among inexperienced ad writers is to write the ad to themselves, rather than to their current and potential customers. Your ads should clearly the benefits (of products and services) to customers, not the benefits to you--clearly state the ads in terms that the customer will value, for example, easy access, low cost, easy to use, reliability, etc. Your ads should answer the customer's question: "What's it it for me?" Your ad should also specify what they are to do next. What action should they take and how do they take it, for example, who do they call and how.

Major Methods of Advertising (Repeatedly Getting Message Out)

Brochures or Flyers--Many desk-top publishing and word-processing software packages can produce highly attractive tri-fold (an 8.5 inch by 11-inch sheet folded in thirds) brochures. Brochures can contain a great deal of information if designed well, and are becoming a common method of advertising.

Direct Mail--Mail sent directly from you to your customers can be highly customized to suit their nature and needs. You may want to build a mailing list of your current and desired customers. Collect addresses from customers by noticing addresses on their checks, asking them to fill out information cards, etc. Keep the list on-line and up-to-date. Mailing lists can quickly become out-of-date. Notice mailings that get returned to you. This should be used carefully and it can incur substantial cost, you don't want to inundate your stakeholders with information so make the most of your message.

E-mail Messages--These can be wonderful means to getting the word out about your business. Design your e-mail software to include a "signature line" at the end of each of your e-mail messages. Many e-mail software packages will automatically attach this signature line to your e-mail, if you prefer.

Magazines--Magazines ads can get quite expensive. Find out if there's a magazine that focuses on your particular industry. If there is one, then the magazine can be very useful because it already focuses on your market and potential customers. Consider placing an ad or writing a short article for the magazine. Contact a reporter to introduce yourself. Reporters are often on the look out for new stories and sources from which to collect quotes.

Newsletters--This can be powerful means to conveying the nature of your organization and its services. Consider using a consultant for the initial design and layout. Today's desktop publishing tools can generate very interesting newsletters quite inexpensively.

Newspapers (major)--Almost everyone reads the local, major newspaper(s). You can get your business in the newspaper by placing ads, writing a letter to the editor or working with a reporter to get a story written about your business. Advertising can get quite expensive. Newspaper are often quite useful in giving advice about what and how to advertise. Know when to advertise--this depends on the buying habits of your customers.

Newspapers (neighbourhood)--Ironically, these are often forgotten in lieu of major newspapers, yet the neighbourhood newspapers are often closest to the interests of the organization's stakeholders.

On-line Discussion Groups and Chat Groups--As with e-mail, you can gain frequent exposure to yourself and your business by participating in on-line discussion groups and chat groups. Note, however, that many groups have strong groundrules against blatant advertising. When you join a group, always check with the moderator to understand what is appropriate.

Posters and Bulletin Boards--Posters can be very powerful when placed where your customers will actually notice them. But think of how often you've actually noticed posters and bulletin boards yourself. Your best bet is to place the posters on bulletin boards and other places which your customers frequent, and always refresh your posters with new and colorful posters that will appear new to passers by. Note that some businesses and municipalities have regulations about the number of size of posters that can be placed in their areas.

Radio Announcements--A major advantage of radio ads is they are usually cheaper than television ads, and many people still listen to the radio, for example, when in their cars. Ads are usually sold on a package basis that considers the number of ads, the length of ads and when they are put on the air.. A major consideration with radio ads is to get them announced at the times that your potential customers are listening to the radio. Telemarketing--The use of telemarketing is on the rise.

Television Ads--Many people don't even consider television ads because of the impression that the ads are very expensive. They are more expensive than most of major forms of advertising. However, with the increasing number of television networks and stations, businesses might find good deals for placing commercials or other forms of advertisements. Television ads usually are priced with similar considerations to radio ads, that is, the number of ads, the length of ads and when they are put on the air.

Web Pages--You probably would not have seen this means of advertising on a list of advertising methods if you had read a list even two years ago. Now, advertising and promotions on the World Wide Web are almost commonplace.

Businesses are developing Web pages sometimes just to appear up-to-date. Using the Web for advertising requires certain equipment and expertise, including getting a computer, getting an Internet service provider, buying (usually renting) a Website name, designing and installing the Website graphics and other functions as needed (for example, an on-line store for e-commerce), promoting the Website (via various search engines, directories, etc.) and maintaining the Website.

Yellow Pages--The Yellow Pages can be very effective advertising if your ads are well-placed in the directory's categories of services, and the name of your business is descriptive of your services and/or your ad stands out (for example, is bolded, in a large box on the page, etc.). The phone company will offer free advice about placing your ad in the Yellow Pages. They usually have special packages where you get a business phone line along with a certain number of ads.

Promotional Activities Through the Media (Reporters, Newspapers, etc.)

Articles that you write--Is there something in your industry or market about you have a strong impression? Consider writing an article for the local newspaper or a magazine. In your article, use the opportunity to describe what you're doing to address the issue through use of your business.

Editorials and letters to the editor--Often, program providers are experts at their service and understanding a particular need in the community; newspapers often take strong interest in information about these needs, so staff should regularly offer articles (of about 200 to 900 words) for publication.

Press kits--This kit is handy when working with the media or training employees about working with the media. The kit usually includes information about your business, pictures, information about your products, commentary from happy customers, etc.

Press releases or news alerts--They alert the press to a major event or accomplishment and requesting, e.g., it get included in the newspaper; they explain who, what, where, why and when; some include pictures, quotes, etc. to make it easier for the reporter to develop an announcement or story.

Public service announcements (PSAs)--Many radio and some television stations will provide public service announcements for nonprofit efforts. Usually, these PSAs are free.

Other Promotional Activities and Events

Annual reports-Disseminate these to key stakeholders; they're ripe with information if they include an overview of your year's activities, accomplishments, challenges and financial status.

Collaboration or strategic restructuring-If you're organization is undertaking these activities, celebrate it publicly.

Networking-Spread the word to peers, professional organizations and those with whom you interact outside the organizations, e.g., educators, consultants, suppliers, clients, etc. (See Networking.)

Novelties--It seems more common to find ads placed on pens and pencils, coffee cups, T-shirts, etc. These can be powerful means of advertising if indeed current and potential customers see the novelties. This condition often implies additional costs to mail novelties, print T-shirts, etc.

Presentations--You're probably an expert at something. Find ways to give even short presentations, for example, at local seminars, Chamber of Commerce meetings, trade shows, conventions, seminars, etc. It's amazing that one can send out 500 brochures and be lucky to get 5 people who respond. Yet, you can give a presentation to 30 people and 15 of them will be very interested in staying in touch with you.

Relationships with key stakeholders--Identify at least one representative from each major stakeholder group and take them to lunch once a year. What seem as short, informal exchanges can cultivate powerful relationships of interest and concern.

Special events--These tend to attract attention, and can include, e.g., an open house, granting a special award, announcing a major program or service or campaign, etc.

Special offers--We see these offers all the time. They include, for example, coupons, discounts, sweepstakes, sales, etc.

8

THE MEDIA ON-LINE

INTRODUCTION

One of the reasons the Internet is such a powerful tool for organizing and advocacy is that it provides an unfiltered means of communication. Whether the issue is air pollution or overpopulation, human rights or union fights, cyberspace is a forum in which activists can communicate their concerns directly to the cyber-public. But Internet outreach is best regarded as a supplement to, not a substitute for, outreach through the media.

Media advocacy remains a powerful way for activists to draw attention to a cause, influence decisions by public agencies and elected officials, or put pressure on a private corporation to change its ways. Activists who use the media effectively have an advantage over those who don't. Unfortunately, it's not always easy to get the media's attention.

The good news is that the Internet has generated a whole new sub-category of media, from flashy Web-based newspapers and magazines to simple electronic newsletters. This means there are more potential outlets to carry your message.

And with E-mail, it's much easier--and far less costly--to send press releases to reporters and editors. This is the case whether they work for a cyberspace publication, or a traditional media outlet.

If you already have a media list, ask the reporters on your list for their E-mail addresses. If they have E-mail, chances are they'll be willing to give you the address.

Once you're compiled an E-mail media list, it's easy to distribute press releases and media advisories at virtually no cost. Whether your community of interest is local, national, or international, on-line distribution of press releases can be effective.

While list software like Majordomo is helpful, it's not essential. With simple-to-use E-mail software like Eudora and Pegasus, you can create a "media" nickname in the mailbox directory. Since the nickname can include multiple E-mail addresses, one "media" nickname is all you'll need to send E-mail to all the reporters and editors you want to reach.

Remember to type the "media" nickname in the "bcc" field of the message header, rather than in the "to" or "cc" field. That way, the press release will be distributed simultaneously to multiple recipients without disclosing any of the recipients' E-mail addresses.

Yes, this is a type of spam. But in my experience, very few reporters complain about receiving unsolicited E-mail press releases. Of course, it's important to send the press release to the right reporter or editor. Someone assigned to the education beat is not going to appreciate receiving a press release about a rally to save the Redwoods.

Getting your press release to the right reporters is just the first step in effective media advocacy. The release itself must be timely, compelling, and concisely written. But that's another subject, which I'll address in another issue of NetAction Notes.

A TOOL KIT OF MEDIA TIPS

One aspect of media advocacy that is often overlooked by activists is talk radio. In addition to a number of syndicated national talk radio programs, many communities have local call-in shows focused on public affairs. These programs offer activists an excellent opportunity to shape public opinion on a wide range of issues.

Chris Roth has compiled a Tool Kit for activists who want to participate in radio and television talk show discussions about free speech. Chris publishes the First Amendment Update, an electronic newsletter that focuses on issues of free speech, artist's rights, and the separation of church and state.

In a recent issue of the First Amendment Update, Chris published an Action Kit of tips for talking to the media. Although the media contact information in the Tool Kit is specific to Wisconsin, where Chris is located, the Tool Kit is an excellent model for activists in other communities. And the tips for talking to the media are applicable anywhere.

In the Tool Kit, Chris has taken the rhetoric of the political right and turned it around. For example, he recommends that First Amendment advocates use words like "snooping," "intolerant," and "extremist" to describe those who favour censorship, while associating support for the First Amendment with words such as "freedom," "liberties," and "Founding Fathers."

FREEDOM OF INFORMATION IN CYBERSPACE

The Freedom of Information Act (FOIA) is an advocacy tool that the media frequently uses, but activists often overlook. FOIA requests to government agencies can turn up all sorts of interesting documents, but patience is required because there are often long delays before documents requested under FOIA rules are provided by government agencies.

Activists interested in filing FOIA requests may find it useful to subscribe to FOI-L, an E-mail list that was started as a service to the National Freedom of Information Coalition.

NFOIC is an alliance of nonprofit state FOI and First Amendment organizations, and academic centers working on First Amendment-related issues.

How to write a conventional press release, where and how to send it?

A news release is known in the news business as a "handout." News people are used to rewriting handouts. They don't get angry if the news release is not a perfect composition, but they do get upset if the facts are not all there. Small papers have few reporters and like to use news releases without re-writing them. Most people can write well enough for small papers. So be humble. Put in all the facts. Write simple sentences.

The First Paragraph

The first paragraph is a summary of what the release is about. In the trade it is called the "lead." These important three lines (never more than four!) determine whether your release sinks or swims.

The Coronado International Historical Pageant, depicting the Hispanic and Indian culture of the Southwest, will be presented free to the public from 10:30 a.m. to 5:15 p.m., on Sunday (April 20) at the Coronado National Mem-orial in Arizona.

This is a fairly routine lead. But notice it answers all the important questions: What? Why? Who? When? Where? It also illustrates another basic rule on the sequence of listing time and place which is called "little time, big time, place." Little time: 10:30 a.m. to 5:15 p.m. Big time: Sunday (April 20) Place: Coronado National Memorial in Arizona.

Alcatraz Island, which has been closed for repairs for two weeks, will be re-opened by the National Park Service for the public on Sunday (April 20), said unit manager Colleen Collins. Reservations at $4.50 each are being accepted for the ferry boat service that begins at 9 a.m. every day, Collins added. The release had two points to make: Alcatraz Island is re-opening AND reservations can now be made. Too much for one sentence. Put them into two sentences. News releases have short paragraphs just like newspapers.

After the Lead Paragraph

Write the rest of your news release in logical order. Simple sentences. Short paragraphs. Use this check list. Did you answer all these questions (if appropriate)? Who? What? When? Where? Why? How? They are known to the old-timers in the business as "The Five W's and How."

Newspaper style dictates certain things in writing. Most of these rules make sense. One rule is: Use the full proper name of a person, or of anything, only once to avoid clutter in the story. Write, for example: The Santa Monica Mountains National Recreation Area, then a short form such as "the area" or "SMMNRA." Another example: "David J. Prosperi," then "Prosperi." There is a rule about numbers that you should follow.

Spell out the numbers one through nine except for dates, time, ages or money. For all other numbers use Arabic numerals: 10, 11, 12, etc. Never write, "11 a.m. in the morning." Write "11 o'clock in the morning" or "11 a.m." Don't be redundant! Again, the principles: "George Berklacy said the Santa Monica Mountains National Recreation Area would open at nine o'clock in the morning." "However, Berklacy later conceded the SMMNRA would not be open until 10 a.m."

Wire services do not use courtesy titles with full names. Dr. is used for initial and subsequent references to physicians, but rarely for others with advanced degrees. Otherwise, for second or further references to the same person use the last name only, without Mr., but with Mrs. or Miss, as appropriate. Ms. is used if that is the known preference of the subject. Exception: Even newspapers that never use courtesy titles in news stories usually include them in obituary reports, as a sign of respect (but a report of a fatality is NOT an obituary). Formal titles are capitalized if they precede a name (Superintendent Ralph Schmidt); lower case if they follow (Ralph Schmidt, superintendent). Titles are lower case when not used with the person's name: "The superintendent of Great Buffalo National Park resigned Wednesday," said William Bigwig, director of the National Park Service.

Note for the Office Secretary: News releases are intended to serve the news media. For that reason, they should conform to wire service (Associated Press or United Press International) rules of style. Correspondence manuals and style guides for research organizations or book publishers should not be used for news releases.

Editors Advisory

The Gatekeeper: Every news organization has a central receiver, a person who screens the flow of incoming releases, calls and visits, determines which have news potential, and directs how the news organization will respond. There are assignment editors, city editors, feature editors, news editors, and more. Radio and television often use the word "director" instead of "editor." Whatever the title, this is the gatekeeper. Learn who it is and cultivate that person.

(No, we don't mean $50 lunches.) Make an appointment to meet him or her professionally. Then, introduce yourself, state your business, and go. Respect busy professionals. After you've made the initial contact, reach these people with simple messages on news release paper. Email versions also must be simple. Graphics and attachments that may cause newsroom delays or disruptions will win no friends. These messages, too, have a variety of names: Editors Advisory, Assignment Memo, Media Advisory, News Memo. This is what gets a reporter to your event. When you want the news media to cover your special event, send them an "editors advisory." If you have an advance news release (and you should) attach a copy to the advisory.

The advisory is particularly valuable in soliciting television coverage. Include a brief description of what will happen and don't forget the visual aspects--what there will be to photograph. If you want advance publicity you will, of course, also send them the news release in a separate envelope.

That's because news media filing systems are usually pretty primitive; your editors advisory and release probably will be put in the "future" file. The editor usually will not make a copy for someone to do a story which would get you advance publicity. If you need advance publicity, send a second release to give you a shot at that, too.

Format for the Editors Advisory

Duncan Morrow (333) 333-3333

Editors Advisory

Event: Secretary of the Interior Opens Coronado International Historical Pageant-a colorful, costumed fiesta of music, song, dance and drama

Time: 11 a.m., Sunday, April 20. (Festival from 10 a.m. to 5 p.m.)

Place: Coronado National Memorial, Hereford, Ariz.

Who: Secretary of the Interior Arnold Andrews and National Park

Service Director Francis Drake: Editors advisories can also be useful at the end of a news release. These are called "trailers." They should be separated from the main text of the release and clearly labelled. Trailer advisories are used to offer supplementary material, related to the release subject. For example, photographs, copies of reports, and review copies of new publications can be offered to the media through such advisories. They must always include clear instructions on how the recipient can obtain the offered items.

Distributing News Releases: The first rule of trash-can avoidance is don't send trash. That is why it is worth taking the time to do a good job. The second rule is don't bury the recipients in a paper blizzard. Use releases only when you have something worth taking an editor's time. There is no quota to be met. An editor who receives too many releases with too little news value soon learns to ignore everything that comes from the same source.

News organizations are trying to interest an audience. If your release will help them do that, they will use it. If it won't, trash it yourself. Honour the role--include a title in every address. In general, use the following titles to address your releases, unless you know a particular organization uses a different title that would serve better:

Daily Newspapers: City Editor

Weekly Newspaper: Editor

Shoppers: Editor

Magazines: Editor

Radio Stations: News Department

Television Stations: News Director

Almost every state has a few newspapers that are circulated over much of the state and that have small bureaus outside of their base city. If such a bureau is near you, put it on the mailing list.

Address the releases to "Bureau Chief" (even if it is a one-person bureau). Don't try to save postage by putting more than one release in the same envelope either. Since different stories are likely to be assigned to different reporters, this may cause one release to be ignored. If you use email, the same principle applies: send separate releases separately.

Timing: Consider to whom you are sending it. Most feature departments (such as travel sections) and magazines have deadlines long before things appear in print. They need to get releases in advance. Weekly papers need releases just before-not just after-their weekly deadlines. The daily media usually have reduced staffs on weekends and are better equipped to act on a release received on a weekday. Time your mailings accordingly.

How to Send e-mail Press Releases. And how NOT to!

We work hard to impress upon our clientele that overuse of the email addresses we've collected is intrusive and offensive. We advocate addressing only those media that are likely to serve an audience that is likely to be interested in the release content. We cannot assure that every client will exercise good judgment.

Fortunately, we also find that most news organizations appreciate thoughtful releases with newsworthy content that can stimulate the research and follow through that are the hallmarks of good journalism, bringing new ideas and issues to an interested readership.

In an era of cost-conscious management, email provides a fast, efficient means of extending the reach of newsroom personnel. At the same time, irrelevant or unwanted material can be instantly deleted from any computer with less effort than it takes to open and discard a traditional, printed release. It is our hope that your future experiences with emailed contributions will be positive and productive.

I once had a fellow who used our newspaper email list (we also offer radio and TV email lists) write to me saying that half of them bounced and that the response was "more than unfriendly". He forwarded all his hate mail to me, along with the supposed undeliverable addresses. Needless to say, I had a minor heart attack and immediately began to find out exactly what he sent, to whom, and how.

I discovered he had pasted all 800 addresses into the TO field of his mail program. Some were separated with commas, some were not. This explained all the bounced mail. It also explained why email that did reach an editor consisted of four pages of nothing but email addresses. Those editors that scrolled down far enough to find his message found a three paragraph teaser-the beginning of a news story. If the editor wanted the rest of the article, they had to go to a website where the full story would be found-but not right away; it would be posted "in a few days". If all that wasn't enough, the letter concluded with a sales pitch to sign up for his "news service" at three cents per word or whatever. This real life example should illustrate a few points.

Know how your mailing software operates. If you have never sent more than one letter at a time, find three friends and do a dry run! Often, pasting a block of names into Carbon Copy will also fill the letter with those names. If you take this cut and paste approach, use Blind Carbon Copy! It has worked for me, but test your own program first. It is really best to have a program that will send individual emails. An observant editor will see that he or she is not a unique recipient if done in any other fashion. However, a press release is not meant to be a personal letter, so this probably shouldn't worry you.

Don't ask a busy editor to go hunting for the news. That's what your concise, well written and pertinent press release should provide. This should be obvious.

And certainly never try to sell an editor something! This should be more than obvious.

Kevin Nunley helps small and mid-sized businesses build effective marketing.

When to Issue a Press Release

Watch for those opportunities when a news release will be appropriate and likely to get into print.

1. Official announcements. Such things as appointments, new services, and organizational accomplishments are regarded as newsworthy.

2. Celebrities and public figures who are doing things with you, your organization or cause.
3. Events such as open houses, tours, award ceremonies, accomplishments, anniversaries, rallies, and debates.
4. Statements that involve you in controversy such as stating your organization's stance on a public issue. Offer a prediction or pass a resolution.
5. Public appearances and big media coverage can interest a reporter. If your work is being featured on "The ABC News," let the newspaper's television editor know about it.
6. Remember to watch for things you can tie-in with. Can you associate yourself with upcoming holidays, public-service projects, and news happenings that are getting lots of attention?
7. Watch for regular newspaper columns that deal with your area of interest. They are especially likely to use your news release, sometimes in its entirety, if your message directly relates to the column's topic. If the paper includes a weekly profile of what's happening on radio, be sure to send them a release anytime you have a scheduled radio interview or when you have recently appeared on the radio with something interesting.

Remember Smaller Newspapers, Newsletters, and E-Zines!

Often times when the big daily paper in your town isn't interested in your story (for example it has too much to do with your business interests with not enough interest for a general audience) consider a more specialized publication.

Trade or industry papers can be excellent for this. The fact that you added a new printer to your printing business is probably of no interest to the big daily paper. However, it might be a good story, accompanied with a photo, for a magazine, newspaper, or newsletter that specializes in the printing industry.

If your business coincides with a minority group or opinion, look for publications which target that smaller group. There's nothing wrong with reaching a smaller audience, especially if that audience is made up of a high percentage of your target prospects.

One of the biggest problems with big mass media (like newspapers and TV) are that they send your message out to just about everybody. It's rare that a business actually needs everybody. Chances are you only sell to specific groups with certain types of interests and needs.

9

Managing the Media

INTRODUCTION

For more than twenty years the Community for Creative Non-Violence has worked in the Nation's Capital on issues of peace and justice. Our work has embraced direct service to homeless and destitute people, as well as resistance to unjust systems and structures. Throughout the years we have tried to raise the consciousness of, and bring needed change to, the world around us through education, direct action, the legal system, and the legislative process. Our most useful tool in this endeavour has been the media.

In Washington, D.C. are more than 3,000 accredited journalists from around the nation and the world. Over the years we have learned many lessons; some particular to this city, others generally applicable everywhere. This handbook is an attempt to communicate these lessons to other activists who may benefit from what we have learned--our successes as well as our failures.

This handbook discusses ways and means of developing experienced media handlers within organizations, creating effective media events, developing relationships with the media, and "managing" the media. You will also find other useful media tips, a section on creating public service announcements (PSAs) and getting them aired, and a discussion from the perspective of a reporter.

A GENERAL PHILOSOPHY

Creating a Media Team: Within the "movement" there is the inclination to be egalitarian with respect to who should deal with the media. While this may create an atmosphere of internal fairness, it will not always get the desired results.

In our early years, we shared responsibility, taking turns as spokesperson, making press calls, and writing press releases, believing that everyone should have an opportunity to be our PR person. As times changed, and we saw our work in increasingly life and death terms, we recognized that those we serve deserve the best we can provide, rather than it offering an "experience" for those who may not be well suited for the job. Lives depend on what we do, and we must never lose sight of that truth.

Very often, those who are on the other side of issues that we support have more money, more power, more access. We can only create an equality of dialogue through our creativity, our commitment, and a professionalism that is equal to theirs. A professional approach to handling the media thus becomes essential. A good, solid media team includes three important roles: a media coordinator, a writer, and a spokesperson. Each is critical to the others, and each is also vital independently to the process of effective media management. Roles may overlap, and often can be handled by the same person, but each position must be covered.

The Media Coordinator

The media coordinator must be someone who is personable, can succinctly articulate the issues, and is willing to spend a great deal of time on the telephone. This person makes sure press releases go out on time, keeps media lists updated, makes press calls, and works actively behind the scenes during events.

The media coordinator should become as well-known behind the camera as the organization's spokesperson is in front of it. One person handling press calls can cultivate important relationships with assignment desk personnel, news producers, and camera people. These people are key to getting the coverage of events you need, and the kind of coverage you want.

Get to know these important people. Always remember that they are people, too. Find out who they are, if they have children, what they enjoy. Make them your best friends, take them to lunch. Develop a personal and working relationship with these pivotal members of the media.

They are used to drones calling with stories, and are disarmed by people who actually care about who they are. Make sure they know you are serious about your issue, but don't be so boring or intense that they don't want to talk to you. Be pushy--but not obnoxious.

The important thing is to make sure that someone who can do something takes your call--that you are not shuffled off to an intern who simply writes down facts and then puts them aside because they don't understand the importance or the urgency of your call. At the same time, interns may someday become assignment desk editors, so don't discount them entirely.

At an event, the media coordinator ensures that all press people receive a statement or handout, that all those present are acknowledged, that all props and sound equipment are in place, that one-on-one interview requests are satisfied, that the photo-op is the one that has been planned beforehand (i.e., that the right people are standing in the right place, etc.), and that the event runs smoothly.

The spokesperson should not have to think about these things--he or she needs to focus attention on what is to be said and not be distracted by details. Again, get to know the people who are there on and off camera. A friendly camera operator can help you get the picture or image you want to project; a producer can spin the story your way.

The Spokesperson

While the spokesperson must be someone who is articulate, he/she should also be more than that. He/She should be a good listener, have camera presence, be well-informed about your issue, be able to think quickly on his/her feet, have credibility, be able to develop a good rapport with a reporter, and be intuitive enough to know when a reporter is not friendly.

Know your interviewers. Do they have a reputation for honest reporting? Are they sympathetic to your issue? Are they fair? Or combative?

If you want to learn to be a good spokesperson, spend time listening to others who are good at the job. Research your issue until you know it inside and out and can hold your own in a conversation or debate. Think through each question that you are likely to be asked, and consider carefully the possible responses. Always be ready to revise and refine. Listen for "good lines" that others may use. Be humble. You always have more to learn

The Writer

Finally, the writer creates the undergirding for all your press events. Clear, concise, effective writing is essential. Because someone is articulate does not mean he/she can write. Have a good editor available to "tighten up" news releases. Everything that is written and released must reflect accurately the position of your organization. Make sure more than one set of eyes from the media team reviews what goes out.

HANDLING THE MEDIA

Never lie to a reporter. If you don't know an answer, simply say so, but add that you will be happy to find out and get back to them. If you are not at liberty to discuss a particular aspect, again, say so, but never lie. Your lie will be discovered, and a good story will turn bad. We learned this the hard way. The New York Times had learned about a discussion we had been having with the White House regarding the resolution of a campaign in which we were involved. They called for confirmation, and because we had not yet resolved things, as we denied the discussion. The reporter found out the truth, and what should have been a victorious and positive story turned into a negative piece. the next day

Don't be forced into saying something you don't want to say. If you don't feel comfortable answering a particular question, answer the one you want asked. Be clear about the point you want to get across. Always bring the discussion back to your points. It is important to realize that much of the substance you want to communicate gets lost. The quote that is inevitably used is the one that is the most colorful. Make it count. Everything else becomes background.

Always remember that your story is in competition with many others. Only seventeen minutes of each half-hour news show is actually news. When you consider time spent on sports, entertainment, weather, and other items the time is even shorter. Your event needs to be interesting enough to capture a few of those precious minutes. This will be discussed in-depth in a later chapter.

We learned much from Ronald Reagan about media management. The most important lesson we learned is that it doesn't matter what you say as long as you say it first. What is printed about an issue first is what the public remembers. Everything from there is catch-up and defense. The Reagan Administration used this tactic masterfully. It became known as "disinformation." We are, of course, not advocating lying. We are suggesting that there are lessons to be learned here.

If you have a story, get it out with your own spin instead of waiting for the other side to do their twist on the truth.

If you know there is going to be a negative story, counter it someplace else first. Some very damaging personal information about a CCNV member was about to be printed in a local paper. We countered by calling another paper and giving them the story on our terms. When the other story appeared, it had been completely discredited already by the story we had planted.

Be smart. Be professional. Learn from others. Invite friendly media people to come to your organization to give workshops on interviews, and other topics. Understand the media people you are trying to influence and make sure they understand you.

CREATING A MEDIA EVENT

We often hear complaints from other activists that the media never covers their events, or that their message is distorted. While reporters often lack depth, or the ability or time to investigate a story thoroughly, quite often the problem is with the source. You must not only be able to communicate your story properly, you must also be able to create an interesting story that is worth telling--and maybe worth retelling. If you are able to generate ongoing debate about your topic, all the better. Controversy is sometimes your best publicity. Three elements can increase the possibility of coverage of your event: interesting people, interesting places, and interesting subjects.

Interesting People

If you don't have a person in your organization who can attract press attention, try to find someone who can. Whether we like it or not, the reality is that some people are media stars. Build relationships with those people, involve them in your issue, and don't hesitate to ask them to stand with you. Stars also come with egos that need to be stroked, and sometimes handling them can be more difficult than handling the media, so beware.

The other type of person who is a magnet for the media is one who can provide the human-interest story--the victim of the policy you are addressing. Be sure the person is a sympathetic person who can present himself/herself well. Interview the individual yourself first. Don't take someone else's word for this person's credibility or believability. Ask all the embarrassing questions that a reporter might ask. Don't let yourself be surprised too late when the camera is rolling. In your pre-interview, spend some time helping the person craft answers that better communicate what he/she is trying to say. If necessary, gently recommend grooming changes. If clothes are needed, help out.

Interesting Places

Whenever possible, hold your event somewhere that will reflect your message. Create an effective backdrop. If you are addressing the lack of affordable housing, then go to empty public housing. If you are speaking about militarism, go to a military base. Try to find a place where members of the press don't usually go, but be sure it isn't so far afield that they can't find it (or want to). We once announced the creation of a new housing and homelessness curriculum for public schools. The president of the National Education Association and the superintendent of our local school district were in attendance, but we held it at a school that was so difficult to find that the press missed the event altogether.

Interesting Subjects

One of the most overlooked and yet important elements in creating an interesting media event is visuals. "Talking heads" at press conferences are boring and commonplace. Find a way to make visible what it is you are trying to communicate. When planning a press event always keep in mind the photo-opt What photo do you want to appear in the paper or on the evening news? Make sure the picture says something. A picture really can be worth a thousand words.

The best visual is the one that requires the fewest words to explain. The more words that are required, the more obtuse the message. During the war in the Middle East we wanted to find a way to remind people that lives were being lost to war daily. We had a long discussion about the nature of that demonstration. First, what was the symbol? Should we mark the dead from other nations? Which location would most clearly communicate the source of the deaths? We ended up with powerful but simple crosses representing each American killed. We planted them on the Ellipse, with the White House in the background. Only one sentence was needed to communicate our message. The photo virtually said it all.

Create a symbol that will represent what you are trying to communicate. While "talking heads" are boring, graphs and charts are only slightly better. A classic Washington media event took place when the Reagan Administration tried to declare catsup a vegetable in the public school lunch program. The sight of members of Congress sitting at a table with a glob of catsup as a side dish still ranks as one of the best news pictures ever taken. Catsup did not become a vegetable.

If there is an event scheduled by someone else that does not portray the truth as you understand it, then don't be afraid to find a way to change the message. One of our favourite examples of this occurred in 1981 when the Reagan Administration announced the first 10% tax cuts through the Kemp-Roth bill. The National Conservative Caucus had planned to serve the world's largest apple pie--symbolizing a bigger piece of the pie for everyone--at the Washington Monument. This was not exactly the truth since only those in upper income brackets would really benefit. Five members of CCNV dressed in large business suits, puffed out with pillows, each wearing large tags that bore the names of Ronald Reagan's rich "kitchen cabinet," ran up on the stage during the speeches and jumped into the pie yelling "It's all for me!" The National Conservative Caucus had done all the groundwork and had gathered the media; we simply redefined the message that was communicated.

If you are planning a large event, find ways to promote it in advance by creating other focal points. It is free advertising, and will build interest in what you really want covered. Maximize every opportunity. Where there isn't an opportunity, create one. A good example of a good opportunity came in 1982 when we planned a luncheon prepared from food that had been pulled from dumpsters or otherwise discarded. Our intention was to promote food salvaging and focus attention on the amount of food wasted regularly in our nation. We planned the lunch for Capitol Hill, and had commitments for attendance from several senators and congressmembers. Two days prior to the feast, we took two members of Congress along with some press people to collect trash with us. With cameras rolling and clicking one elected official hoisted himself into a dumpster and began to pull out food. That picture went around the nation, and set the scene for our message to be delivered two days later.

Timing for a media event is critical to maximizing its potential. As a general rule, the best times for an event are Monday through Thursday from 10 a.m. until 12 noon. Morning hours will guarantee that deadlines are met, and will allow for further development of the story. Some newspapers do not publish on weekends, which means Friday events won't be covered. Stories covered on the evening news quite often have a bonus in weekday morning coverage as well. News offices usually have short crews on weekends, and simply do not have the personnel available at that time to cover your story. In addition, reporters who are regularly assigned to cover particular issues are often off on weekends. Finally, weekends have fewer news viewers.

Sometimes, however, it is worth taking a calculated risk in timing. For instance, CCNV holds an annual Thanksgiving dinner for the homeless on the grounds of the U.S. Capitol.

We schedule it in late afternoon to encourage live television coverage. News on weekends and holidays is often so slow that news directors are looking for stories.

One of the best news events I can remember recently revolved around a fund raising dinner for a boarder baby project. Two Motown groups flew in for the event, scheduled in the evening. The organization held a noon press conference at the home for boarder babies with the president of the non-profit, the celebrities, and some beautiful gurgling babies. After the speeches were made, the singers held the babies and crooned songs in an impromptu concert. The press ate it up.

The best of all media events has plenty of action and creativity. Find the ironies in situations. Inject humor when it is appropriate. Deliver your message with vigor and enthusiasm.

CREATING A PRESS LIST

Maintain two press lists: a press mailing list, and a press call list.

The press mailing list should contain the name of the publication, station, or network, its address, and the names of people that you know at each location. While it is important to mail releases to the assignment desk, it is also important to target specific reporters with whom you may have already developed an ongoing relationship. It is all right to send multiple releases to the same place. Your story may not interest one person, but hook someone else.

If you have a computerized press mailing list, organize it according to type and reach of the media organization (i.e., local, national, religious, women, etc.), so that you can target specific areas when necessary. For instance, your story may be strictly a local story, and sending a press release to all of the national media outlets is inappropriate. Every area of the country falls into a media market. Large cities and the surrounding suburbs make up their own media markets, while rural areas may contain a vast geographic area. For instance, the Washington market includes Washington, D.C., and the areas immediately surrounding the beltway. It does not include Baltimore, which is its own market. Find out the geographic area that your media market covers.

Media markets are usually served by more than one television, radio, or wire service, or "news feed." When local stations are small they can rarely afford to have crews or reporters traveling to cover stories, so they contract with a larger service to get stories for them in other cities. For instance Cox Broadcasting serves Dayton, Atlanta, and Pittsburgh. Capitol Broadcast covers stories for the Hartford, Atlanta, and Philadelphia areas.

Learn about these media services in your area. Also find out which other areas they serve. Add them to your press lists. Your story may have interest in another area where a similar problem is being addressed. If there is some way you can tie your story into a story in another city, it is all the better.

A press call list is also essential. Always keep it handy. Your call list will be considerably smaller than your mailing list. CCNV maintains a mailing list of 1,800, but has a call list of just about 100.

Also organize your call list by category of media organization. Break down this list even further than the mailing list (i.e., wire services, local newspapers, local television, radio stations, network news, etc.). Again, this facilitates the press call process. Call lists should include the agency name, phone number, fax number, assignment desk names, reporters' names, special news areas they cover, and individual direct dial and home numbers when available.

Always keep press mailing lists and call lists up to date. Add new names as you meet new people. Your media coordinator should take names of producers and reporters at press events and make sure those names get added to your lists.

PRESS RELEASES AND CALLS

Timing the Press Release and Call

A press release can serve a number of purposes. It is usually used to announce an event but can be used as a handout, can become a position paper, or can be used to educate the media about a topic. In any case, it is always important to have something in writing.

Timing the release is important. If your event is planned well in advance it is good to mail it out at least a week ahead to ensure its inclusion on calendars. Sometimes, however, this is not possible. If a short lead time is all you have, faxing the release works just as well. When you must fax the release, be sure to target the person most likely to be interested in the event, since it is difficult to send to everyone on your list. In some cases, there is no time for a press release at all. If you plan a clandestine action, or if something develops quickly and unpredictably, there may be only enough time for a press call as you walk out the door.

On occasions when we wanted to surprise someone, and could not release the information early, we took lots of quarters and a press list with us and called from a pay phone as our action was in progress. Sometimes, if we have been working with a particular reporter we feel we can trust, we release the information in advance to that person only, with the understanding that it must not be leaked to others. On other occasions we have called the media in advance and suggested that they would get a good story and picture if they appeared at a certain corner at a certain time. Because we have enough credibility with our local media, and because we don't use that tactic often, they usually show up.

A good validation of that strategy happened when we announced a march on City Hall. I called my friends in the media and told them that there would be something else that they would not want to miss--a surprise. When everyone was in place, two members of CCNV climbed out the 12th floor window of the hotel across the street and rappelled off the side of the building with a 100 foot banner. Nobody was disappointed. In situations like that it is critical that a media coordinator be on hand to direct the cameras in the right direction. Don't forget, nobody knows what they are looking for, or what to expect.

All press releases should be followed with a press call. Be thorough with your calls. This is when your past dealings with producers and assignment desk personnel are important. Always ask for the person you know best. Be persistent. Just because your story was not covered after your last call, or even the last ten calls, does not mean that it will not be covered this time. Sometimes it depends on what else newsworthy is going on at the time, but good, persistent press work tends to have a cumulative effect.

Writing the Release

Press releases are the first encounter a media outlet will have with your event. While you want to be thorough and include all the information, and the underlying data, you also need to be succinct. In some large media markets, hundreds of press releases can cross an assignment desk each day. If your release is too wordy, it will likely be ignored.

The first paragraph should include the "five W's"--who, what, where, when, and why. Don't forget, your first goal is to get them to come to your event. If you have a high-profile person who will attract media, include his name in this first paragraph.

The next paragraphs should include an expansion on the purpose of the event, and some history of what led up to it. Don't assume that the person who will be reading the release will necessarily be up to date on recent developments in your issue. If the location of your event is significant, include a discussion of its importance. It is also important to include some brief background material on any special people who will be in attendance.

The release should include a quote from the spokesperson for your organization. Try to be pithy, clear, and to the point. This will very often be the quote used in the print media. Make it count.

Finally, include a brief description of your organization. This is particularly important if you are a new organization, a re-formed organization, or as yet unknown to the media.

Before you write your release, sit down and list the points you wish to make. Be clear. Don't ramble. While you need to include enough background information to educate, you don't need to say everything in the release. That is the purpose of the press event.

The form of the press release can vary. There are, however, a few elements common to all press releases. Always begin with the date the information can be released. Somewhere at the top of the page type "PRESS RELEASE" several times. All press releases end with "# # #" or "-30-" typed in the middle of the page toward the bottom of the release. Be sure to include contact names (it is best to have two names) and their phone numbers. Press releases should always be printed on your letterhead.

Press Calls

In many ways the press calls you make are more important than the press release. Although it is critical to have a written press statement that can be delivered or faxed upon request, it is during the call that you have the opportunity to really sell your story. In addition, press calls give the assignment desk person or the reporter the opportunity to ask questions, clarify the issue, and develop the "background" information that will be necessary to give depth to your story. It is during press calls that important relationships begin to be forged with the media outlet.

Be sensitive to the people on the other end of the telephone. If they seem rushed, don't keep them any longer than you need to. If they seem to have more time, chat them up.

Think through what you have to say very carefully before you ever lift the receiver. Write it down or rehearse it if necessary. Start with the less important calls in order to smooth and develop your "rap."

Be succinct and clear, yet prepared to go into details if there is an opportunity. Always get the "who," "what," "where," and "when" out first. While the "why" is important, your first purpose is to get the news crew to the event.

Learn the names of assignment desk editors, and always keep them updated on your press list. When developing your list it may be useful to call the news outlets and get the names of these important people (weekend assignment editors are often different than weekday editors). Ask for them by name. You are less likely to get shuffled off to an intern if you can ask for a specific person. Always try to work with the same person--this is how relationships develop.

A typical press call should begin like this: "Hello, this is Carol Fennelly at the Community for Creative Non-Violence. I'm calling to be sure you received the press release we sent about the rally to oppose the closing of city shelters scheduled for Monday, December 2 at 12 noon at the District Building." Be sure to leave your telephone number so you can be reached for follow-up questions.

If you can go into greater detail, go for it. But again, be sensitive to the person on the other end of the line. If the reporter seems to be rushing, don't irritate him/her with more verbiage. Your message is out, and they will call back when they have more time.

If your press release has been lost among the hundreds that have crossed their desk, fax or deliver another immediately. Have an assistant ready to get it out quickly, while you are still on their mind.

Once you have made a few initial practice calls, follow this procedure. Start with the wire services (i.e., Associated Press and United Press International) since they can rapidly get the news out to everybody else. Follow those calls with television stations, since they have more staff to try to get to the location of your media function. Those contacts should be followed with calls to newspapers next, then radio stations. Don't forget those independent news feeds mentioned earlier.

Calls should always be made the morning of the event. You can generally get a good sense of who to expect to show up. If you have enough time, calls should also be made one or two days before as well. If we have a large event scheduled, and know well in advance that it is going to occur, we send out a press release the week before, make calls two days prior, and the morning of the event.

Be thorough. What does not get a response the first time, only builds for your next call. No call is a wasted call. Each one helps keep your cause in the forefront.

COMMUNITY FOR CREATIVE NON-VIOLENCE PRESS RELEASE

Party for Homeless People

The Community for Creative Non-Violence is hosting two parties for homeless people on December 24. The first a party for homeless families, will be held at The Great Hall of the Hubert Humphrey Building at 3rd and Independence from 2:00-3:30 p.m. The second party is for the single residents of CCNV's Federal City Shelter, 425 Second Street, NW, and is scheduled for 5:00 7:00 p.m.

Boxing great Sugar Ray Leonard, Senator Jesse Jackson, and Washington Redskins Darrell Green, Ron Hiddleton,

Raleigh McKenzie, Ed Simmons, George Starke and Ricky Sanders are expected to make appearances at the party for homeless children and their mothers. Mayor Sharon Pratt Kelly and Secretary of Health and Human Services Louis Sullivan have been invited to attend as well. Polaroid has contributed film and cameras to allow the children to take away pictures of themselves with their favourite athlete or politician.

In addition, food will be served, gifts will be distributed clowns and magicians will entertain, and performers will present a show for the children. The District Government will provide transportation for the families from the shelters it operates to the HHS building.

At the party for the 1500 single adults housed at CCNV's Federal City Shelter choirs and bands will perform, Senator Jesse Jackson will visit, gifts will be distributed, and a special dinner will be served.

"For those who are homeless, Christmas is a time of enormous emptiness and loneliness and pain. It is a time of memories of better days. A time of hopes and dreams abandoned, just as they themselves, have been abandoned," said CCNV spokesperson Carol Fennelly. " Christmas Eve--the night of great and joyful expectations--is particularly difficult for those who little to expect but more of the same. That is why we have had this party for the last ten years."

The PSA

The public service announcement serves many purposes. It raises consciousness, educates, announces an event, or generates funds or other material needs. Depending upon the type of PSA you create, a radio or TV station may air it at no cost.

Most stations have an employee assigned to deal with public affairs. That person is responsible for deciding which public service announcements get on the air. When you have a PSA, contact that person well in advance to find out what kind of lead time they may need. If you are producing a taped PSA find out what format they need (i.e., television stations usually want 3/4" or 1 " tape, while radio stations may want reel-to-reel or cassette). Stations will usually only run 10, 30, or 60 second announcements. Prepare them in all three lengths.

If your public service announcement endorses a candidate, specific legislation, or promotes merchandise, it is considered advertising, and you will be charged a fee. If you are simply educating, you can usually find a station to air it at no cost. In addition, stations often have community billboards to advertise events, volunteer needs, or material needs (although they may not be willing to make fundraising pleas).

Community billboard-type announcements are better submitted in writing for announcers to read on the air. Also, if you do not have the ability to prepare your own taped PSA, write it down (again, in 10, 30 and 60 second versions) and submit it. Be sure to read it out loud to verify the length of each version.

Here is an example:

60 second: The Community for Creative Non-Violence is holding a fundraising party and auction at the Hard Rock Cafe on Tuesday, November 12, from 8 p.m. until midnight. Live music will be provided by Bo Diddley, Jr. and Jennifer Ferguson. A delicious free buffet, cash bar, and a live and silent auction are also planned. Actors Armand Asante and Michael O'Keefe, Channel 7's Paul Berry, and Washington Redskin's Darrell Green and George Stark will be guest auctioneers. Auction items include a dress worn by former Supreme Mary Wilson, a jacket worn by Sugar Ray Leonard during the third Duran fight, and articles of clothing from the entire cast of "L.A. Law." The Hard Rock Cafe is located at 10th and E Streets, NW. Tickets are $ 15 and available at the door or at Ticket Master. For more information contact CCNV at 202-393-1909.

30 second: The Community for Creative Non-Violence is holding a fundraising party and auction at the Hard Rock Cafe on Tuesday, November 12, from 8 p.m. until midnight. Live music, a free buffet, cash bar, and a live and silent auction are planned. Armand Asante, Michael O'Keefe, Paul Berry, Darrell Green, and George Stark will be guest auctioneers. The Hard Rock Cafe is located at 10th and E Streets, NW. Tickets are $ 15. Contact CCNV at 393-1909.

10 second: The Community for Creative Non-Violence is holding a fundraising party and auction at the Hard Rock Cafe on Tuesday, November 12, from 8 p.m. until midnight. The Hard Rock Cafe is located at 10th and E Streets, NW.

Creating a public service announcement that educates or raises consciousness is a little more difficult and requires a more thoughtful approach. These are best pre-taped in order to get the desired effect.

First, you must identify the particular audience you wish to reach. Is it middle America? Working people? Women? Parents? It is important to frame your message in a way that will reach that population? What are their concerns in relation to your issue? What myths or misconceptions do you need to overcome? What action do you hope to get them to take?

10

The Basics of Press Relations

Like fund raising, press relations is an ongoing cultivation process. Your organization's strategy for press coverage needs to go beyond trying to land one big story; you want the press to know that you are THE organization to contact whenever they are doing a story on a subject that relates to your organization's work, and that you are a reliable source for information and stories. In short, you want to be quoted or referenced in a variety of stories, not just one.

Therefore, don't think that every press release is going to result in press coverage--it's not. But sustaining regular press contacts will build recognition of your organization among reporters, and the result will be ongoing payoffs down the road. As coverage for your organization is generated, you won't just be reaching new audiences--you will also be reaching current volunteers, supporters (including donors) and clients, reminding them of what your organization is doing and what they have chosen to be a part of.

The following suggestions are low-cost or no-cost activities. They don't require money to undertake, as much as they require time and commitment.

- Make a commitment to return calls from the media immediately. Whether it is a large newspaper or a small community radio show, if a representative tries to reach you, always call or email that person back immediately. The person contacting you could be on deadline, and if they don't reach you immediately, they might move on to another organization.

- Make a commitment to be honest with the press. Treat the press the way you want to be treated. The moment the press decides you aren't telling them the truth, they will deliver a public relations nightmare to you and your initiative. That doesn't mean going out and telling the press every bad thing happening at your initiative, but it does mean answering press questions to the BEST of your abilities-and that can include this phrase: "I do not have a comment on that."
- Next: is your mission statement the perfect, brief description of your organization? If not, revise it before you approach the press. If you don't write a good, brief description of your organization and have such displayed prominently on your Web site and letterhead, in press releases and brochures, etc., the press will make up one themselves--and it may or may not be accurate. As a followup to the previous step: everyone at your organization should be able to recite that mission statement from memory. If it's too long for paid staff, volunteers and board members to easily remember, it's too long for the press to remember as well.
- Media relations needs to be fully supported by everyone at your organization, and you need policies and procedures around your organization's press relations. Answering these questions is a start in forming your policies:
    * Who is responsible for media relations at your organization (writing press releases, answering calls from the press, inviting press to events, etc.)? Does the person who answers the phone know to refer ALL calls from the press to that staff member?

* Do all paid staff members and volunteers (including board members) know exactly what to do if they are contacted by a press representative? (do they talk with that person and then let the organization's media contact person know they have done so, or, do they refer the reporter to the media contact person FIRST before any conversations/interviews take place?) Decide on a policy, one way or another, and make sure it is communicated to everyone.

* Other than the press relations contact person, who at your organization needs to know that a photographer or camera crew is showing up at your organization or event? The press relations person should brief everyone at the organization as quickly as possible if a photographer or camera crew is on its way.

* Should the press contact person be present at all interviews? That's up to you. My personal rule when in charge of media relations is that I am to be present at all media interviews unless I am absolutely certain that the interviewee will be able to answer all questions, that he or she feels comfortable with my not being there, and I know the interviewer well. That policy comes from trying to balance giving a person enough "space" with providing proper support.

* As a result of your media outreach activities, what exactly do you want to happen? More people at an event? A particular group of people at an event (such as potential donors, government officials, local religious leaders)? An increase in the number of on-line references to your organization? An increase in recognition of your organization among the general public? Know your goals, think about how your media outreach

activities could reach those goals, and think about ways to measure your success.

- Identify all area media outlets, long before you ever have the need to contact them. You want the names, postal addresses, phone numbers, fax numbers, and email address of all local daily and weekly newspapers, all TV stations, all radio stations, all organizations and editors that maintain event calendars (such as a tourism board that serves your area, or the nearest consulates or embassies of other countries), all press bureau offices for national or major regional media in your area, and all TV programs, radio programs and specific beat reporters that would be interested in your initiative's work in particular. If you are in a rural area, also identify the major media outlets for the nearest metropolitan area. You can use Google or Yahoo to compile this information, as well as contacting other organizations for advice.

You don't necessarily have to have reporter's names-sending something to "Attention Calendar Editor" at a newspaper will get to the right person as quickly as putting that person's name on it. And given the high turnover in media, it's certainly easier to maintain your database of media contacts this way. Also, look for reporters at national media outlets who cover your specific geographic area or cover a topic that is closely aligned with your initiative's mission. Regularly monitor free on-line news sources, such as YahooNews, to find such reporters. Don't wait until you have a press release to send to gather this contact information!

- Do you know how to write a press release? If not, type in these words:

SAMPLE PRESS RELEASE

into Google; you will get a long list of web sites that feature sample press releases. For your press release contact information, put your cell phone as well as your office phone, if you are not in your office most of the time.

- Do NOT contact ALL media outlets EVERY TIME you send a press release (if such is more than every other month). If you do, you will overwhelm the organization, and reporters and editors will stop reading your materials. Also, some publications are highly-focused: a weekly neighbourhood or community paper may interested only in activities that DIRECTLY and OBVIOUSLY involve their particular community or population served. Therefore, you may have to tailor press releases to these publications to illustrate this connection clearly.

  Who gets what information, and when?

  The following is a general overview, but you will need to tailor this for your own organization's events and resources, as well as per your goals for media outreach. For instance, I directed public relations activities for a professional association in Austin, Texas for two years; this organization had a limited space for its monthly meetings. My first efforts more than filled the room--much to everyone's discomfort. The association did not want to move to a bigger space and could not provide microphones for speakers. So I scaled back by outreach efforts, generating enough attendance just to fill the room and meet the annual membership goals.

  Working with other staff members, develop an outreach calendar: What are the dates of events your organization will sponsor in the next six months? What about events that will involve your Executive Director or other key staff (a high-profile speaking engagement to a key group or conference, for instance)? What about the launch of a new program or service? The launch of your annual fund raising campaign?

Once you've developed this calendar of events, you can set your dates to contact the media. Your press release "send" schedule should follow this basic model:

* Calendar editors (including those that manage on-line calendars) get press releases that announce events, workshops, etc. These should be sent two-three weeks in advance for daily and weekly publications; they should be sent at least eight weeks in advance for monthly publications.

* Assignment editors at TV stations get press releases two weeks in advance that announce events you think would provide good visuals for the news. Remember that TV stations are looking for lively visuals (faces and movement). You should also fax a reminder to the assignment editor 12-24 hours before such an event--a one page fax with just the who, what, why, where, when, how, a contact name and why this event is particularly "filmable" (this is one of those cases where a fax is still better than email).

* Beat reporters (people who are assigned to a particular subject or issue area, such as education, entertainment, senior issues, sports, etc.) should get press releases ONLY for events, workshops or services that relate to their particular focus. Send these two-four weeks in advance.

* In urban areas, most radio stations have a music format, and have very limited time for public service announcements. Send your press releases to only those radio stations that feature regular news times, audio event calendars or public affair shows, following the sending guidelines above. For other radio stations, consider event partnerships; are you hosting an event that would be a good place for a radio station to set up a live broadcast? Or are you trying to target a particular

community or population that also makes up most of an audience of a particular radio station (for instance, if an organization is hosting a conflict resolution workshop for youth, perhaps the radio station that teenagers listen to most in the area would be willing to sponsor this event and promote it on their station)?

- In addition to announcing events, you can send press releases to:
  - announce new activities, the latest results of or changes in your programs and services
  - highlight particularly effective, unique, innovative or interesting volunteer activities
  - announce how a particular piece of pending or recently-passed legislation will affect your organization and those it serves
  - announce the results of your latest fund-raising efforts, a new grant you have just received, or a partnership you have formed with another organization/other organizations
  - announce your latest annual financial report
  - announce awards your organization is giving or receiving
  - announce staff changes
  - announce an impending visit to your organization by an internationally-recognized expert
  - acknowledge a particular day of focus that relates to your organization and its work

    (for instance, if you are an environmental organization, send a press release relating to Earth Day, about two weeks before the day itself; or, if you are an organization with a program or programs focused on women, send a press release relating to International Women's Day)

- Non-press organizations and other non-press representatives should also get your organization press releases (as appropriate); this is how you will build a public reputation and become associated with public policy issues that might affect your organization's target population. As a result, these organizations may start directing calls from the press to you when they get them, as appropriate:
  * city (mayor, council people), county, state (legislators) and federal officials (congresspeople and senators) that represent your area
  * chambers of commerce (most areas are served by more than one--there's the main one, but there also might be a Black chamber, a women's chamber, etc.), tourist association, arts council, etc.
  * send press releases announcing major events or activities to local consulates or embassies representing other organizations (they might refer foreign press to you)
  * if you are in the USA: the United Way (even if you are NOT a United Way agency)
  * nonprofit development or support centers that serve your area
  * nonprofit and public sector agencies in your area with a similar focus
  * professional associations and civic groups
  * university departments that have studies that focus on the same areas served by your mission; for instance, if you serve children and youth, send information to the teacher-training school within a university
- Should you send press releases primarily via email, fax, phone calls or post? It depends on your resources, the news you are providing, and who you are

contacting. Email is less of a cost than the post or fax, but some reporters are so overwhelmed by junk mail, solicitations and email press releases that your information could get lost in the sea of cyberspace. I got my start in press relations in the pre-Internet days (in fact, in the pre-fax days), sending press releases primarily by postal mail, but I do use email now, most of the time, and with excellent results. I supplement this with phone calls and/or faxes to reporters when I'm targeting someone in particular for coverage. Different situations call for different communications methods, and I'm constantly altering my delivery methods based on the ever-changing times and the results of my most-recent efforts. I can't give you an absolute formula; you are going to have to figure this one out for yourself.

- Make sure the press see your executive director and other key staff and board members as accessible. For instance, the head of your organization should have lunch or dinner occasionally, one-on-one, with key local reporters, not necessarily to pitch stories or to do an interview, but just to network and cultivate a relationship. However, staff members should NOT consider these meetings off the record; they need to watch what they say and conduct themselves as representatives of the organization at all times.
- Consider arranging with a local or national newspaper for your executive director or another key representative to write an editorial or commentary for the paper in conjunction with a current "hot" issue or a day with special significance. You can ghost-write the column with him or her. The editorial will probably have to be submitted three weeks before the day the column is to run.
- Consider making an exclusive pitch to a reporter. For instance, if there is a fantastic, exceptional success

story regarding someone your organization has helped, you could call a trusted press person with whom you have a good relationship, and offer to set up an interview and photo opportunity regarding this person only for that particular press person.

- If your organization feels an event is inappropriate for a camera crew (for instance, a dress rehearsal for a play the night before opening, or a group counseling session with children), what alternative can you give the crew? Always have alternatives ready when a film crew calls.
- Also, ALWAYS notify people they are going to be (or might be) photographed or filmed BEFORE it happens! You don't want someone throwing a fit for the evening news. If children will be present, get parental permission first!
- Not all press relations is about good news: you may also have to engage in press and other outreach to counter misunderstandings, rumors and myths, or to counter on-line criticism. That will be much easier to do if you have followed the above guidelines and established a good, ongoing relationship with the press.

Those are the basics--they will get you started on the road to building a reputation with the press and getting media coverage. There's much more you can do, ofcourse, but these basic activities will build a great foundation for expanded efforts. Note how many of these activities have to do with human contacts, commitment to outreach, and always having information available for the press, rather than what tools you use.

EVALUATE AND CELEBRATE YOUR EFFORTS

Evaluate your media outreach efforts every few months: Are stories being generated? Are press people attending your events? Are more people attending your events or calling your organization? The person who answers your phone, or anyone who signs anyone up for an activity at your organization (volunteers, donors, people who attend events, etc.), should ask these people, at the time they are signing up, how they heard about your organization, the activity or the event. This will help you to learn how effective your outreach activities are, and help you plan strategically for the future.

Also, make sure other staff members know the results of your efforts:

- Distribute copies of all articles that appear about your organization, positive or negative, in newspapers or on-line, to all staff and board members. As resources allow and as appropriate, also send copies of stories to volunteers, donors and customers/clients.
- Find space in a public area at your organization or a place that staff frequent (the break room or a hallway, for instance) for a "brag board," where you will post articles about your organization that are published in newspapers or on-line. (NOTE: I once got a raise because the Executive Director stood in front of the brag board and was stunned that so much press had been generated; he'd seen the articles as they had come out, but seeing three months of positive newspaper articles posted on a wall made a BIG impression).
- Also watch the "Letters to the Editor" column for things that might relate to your organization, and distribute them appropriately. If your Executive Director or other staff member writes a letter on behalf of your organization (with pre-approval from the organization, ofcourse), make sure all staff and board members get copies (and, as appropriate, make copies for volunteers, donors and clients, particularly if it is rebutting a negative article).

- A notice should go out to all staff and board members if a TV, radio or on-line broadcast is going to feature on your organization (more than just a mention of the dates and times of an event).
- A notice should go out to all staff, board members, volunteers, donors and customers/clients if there is a partnership with a particular media outlet for an event your organization is sponsoring.

THE ROLE OF VOLUNTEERS IN MEDIA RELATIONS

Can volunteers help with media relations?

Should volunteers be involved with media relations?

The answer to both is yes--but with some cautions!!!

Many organizations are too small to hire a full-time paid media relations person and, therefore, must rely on volunteers to help with media relations. Great assignments for volunteers in this role, including pro-bono consultants, include:

- researching media (looking for and documenting local, regional, national and international media contacts)
- monitoring media (using tools like Yahoo News Search) to find stories about your organization, or reporters doing stories relating to your organization's interest that could be good to approach)
- drafting press releases
- suggesting ideas for press releases
- drafting press strategies

It's preferable for a full-time or part-time paid staff person, who is in the office regularly and frequently, to be the media contact person, however, as most volunteers are not in an organization's offices regularly and frequently, and therefore may not be around if a press person calls. If you have no choice but to have a volunteer to be your media contact person, make sure that person can make the necessary time commitment, every day and for a substantial length of time, to fulfill all activities associated with basic media outreach that has been defined here.

EVERYONE IS NOT REACHED BY THE PRESS

Reaching the press is vital for your organization, but it must be done with the realization that not everyone is reached by the press. Not everyone reads, or has access, to newspapers or on-line news, and not everyone has access, or listens, to radio, TV or on-line broadcasts. Representatives from your organization will have to reach out, often face-to-face, to conferences, communities of faith, farmer's associations, women's cooperatives, professional associations, schools, universities, student groups, informal groups and various other associations, formal or not, to get your organization's messages out and understood to everyone you need to reach. You will also have to think about posters and handouts, and in some cases, even live performance methods (theatre, dance, puppets, etc.), in order to reach everyone with your information.

Press relations is oh-so-important, but remember that it's only one part of your overall community outreach.

Other resources:

- The Care and Feeding of the Press by Esther Schindler and the members of the Internet Press Guild is a good guide to people who pitch stories to the on-line press. It's from the press's point of view, and offers good advice about writing your press releases and making your pitch.
- Outreach Via the Internet for

Not-for-Profit or Public Sector Organizations

It's more than just putting up a Web site; it involves finding and posting to appropriate Internet discussion groups, sending emails to current and potential customers, perhaps even starting your own on-line community.... it's pro-active, interactive and ongoing.

- What are good blog topics for mission-based organizations?

The word "blog" is short for "web log", and means keeping a journal or diary on-line. Blogging is NOT a new concept--people have been doing it long before it had a snazzy media label. The appeal of blogging for an on-line audience is that it's more personal and less formal than other information on a web site. Readers who want to connect with an organization on a more personal level, or who are more intensely interested in an organization than the perhaps general public as a whole, love blogs. Blogs can come from your Executive Director, other staff members, volunteers, and even those you serve. Content options are many, and this list reviews some of your options.

- Strategic communications toolkit

The digital media environment brings new potential for partnerships and collaborations, inviting qualitatively different relationships between organisations and their constituencies, members and donors. Non-profit leaders need credible, succinct information to meet the challenges of the digital age. The Benton Foundation capacity building project documented best practices and lessons learned by non-profits about the impact, successes, failures and struggles in using the strategic communications toolkit. This toolkit catalogues valuable lessons on what it takes to design and fund an effective communications technology strategy, including planning, audience development, message shaping, evaluation and funding.

PUBLIC RELATIONS SPECIALISTS

Significant Points:

- Although employment is projected to grow faster than average, keen competition is expected for entry-level jobs.

- Opportunities should be best for college graduates who combine a degree in public relations, journalism, or another communications-related field with a public relations internship or other related work experience.
- Creativity, initiative, and the ability to communicate effectively are essential.

Nature of the Work

An organization's reputation, profitability, and even its continued existence can depend on the degree to which its targeted "publics" support its goals and policies. Public relations specialists-also referred to as communications specialists and media specialists, among other titles-serve as advocates for businesses, nonprofit associations, universities, hospitals, and other organizations, and build and maintain positive relationships with the public.

As managers recognize the importance of good public relations to the success of their organizations, they increasingly rely on public relations specialists for advice on the strategy and policy of such programs.

Public relations specialists handle organizational functions such as media, community, consumer, industry, and governmental relations; political campaigns; interest-group representation; conflict mediation; and employee and investor relations. They do more than "tell the organization's story." They must understand the attitudes and concerns of community, consumer, employee, and public interest groups and establish and maintain cooperative relationships with them and with representatives from print and broadcast journalism.

Public relations specialists draft press releases and contact people in the media who might print or broadcast their material. Many radio or television special reports, newspaper stories, and magazine articles start at the desks of public relations specialists. Sometimes the subject is an organization and its policies toward its employees or its role in the community. Often the subject is a public issue, such as health, energy, or the environment, and what an organization does to advance that issue.

Public relations specialists also arrange and conduct programs to keep up contact between organization representatives and the public. For example, they set up speaking engagements and often prepare speeches for company officials. These media specialists represent employers at community projects; make film, slide, or other visual presentations at meetings and school assemblies; and plan conventions. In addition, they are responsible for preparing annual reports and writing proposals for various projects.

In government, public relations specialists-who may be called press secretaries, information officers, public affairs specialists, or communication specialists-keep the public informed about the activities of agencies and officials. For example, public affairs specialists in the U.S. Department of State keep the public informed of travel advisories and of U.S. positions on foreign issues. A press secretary for a member of Congress keeps constituents aware of the representative's accomplishments.

In large organizations, the key public relations executive, who often is a vice president, may develop overall plans and policies with other executives. In addition, public relations departments employ public relations specialists to write, research, prepare materials, maintain contacts, and respond to inquiries.

People who handle publicity for an individual or who direct public relations for a small organization may deal with all aspects of the job. They contact people, plan and research, and prepare materials for distribution. They also may handle advertising or sales promotion work to support marketing efforts.

WORKING CONDITIONS

Some public relations specialists work a standard 35-to 40-hour week, but unpaid overtime is common. Occasionally, they must be at the job or on call around the clock, especially if there is an emergency or crisis. Public relations offices are busy places; work schedules can be irregular and frequently interrupted. Schedules often have to be rearranged so that workers can meet deadlines, deliver speeches, attend meetings and community activities, and travel.

TRAINING, OTHER QUALIFICATIONS, AND ADVANCEMENT

There are no defined standards for entry into a public relations career. A college degree combined with public relations experience, usually gained through an internship, is considered excellent preparation for public relations work; in fact, internships are becoming vital to obtaining employment. The ability to communicate effectively is essential. Many entry-level public relations specialists have a college major in public relations, journalism, advertising, or communication. Some firms seek college graduates who have worked in electronic or print journalism. Other employers seek applicants with demonstrated communication skills and training or experience in a field related to the firm's business-information technology, health, science, engineering, sales, or finance, for example.

Many colleges and universities offer bachelor's and postsecondary degrees in public relations, usually in a journalism or communications department. In addition, many other colleges offer at least one course in this field. A common public relations sequence includes courses in public relations principles and techniques; public relations management and administration, including organizational development; writing, emphasizing news releases, proposals, annual reports, scripts, speeches, and related items; visual communications, including desktop publishing and computer graphics; and research, emphasizing social science research and survey design and implementation. Courses in advertising, journalism, business administration, finance, political science, psychology, sociology, and creative writing also are helpful. Specialties are offered in public relations for business, government, and nonprofit organizations.

Many colleges help students gain part-time internships in public relations that provide valuable experience and training. Membership in local chapters of the Public Relations Student Society of America (affiliated with the Public Relations Society of America) or in student chapters of the International Association of Business Communicators provides an opportunity for students to exchange views with public relations specialists and to make professional contacts that may help them find a job in the field. A portfolio of published articles, television or radio programs, slide presentations, and other work is an asset in finding a job. Writing for a school publication or television or radio station provides valuable experience and material for one's portfolio.

Creativity, initiative, good judgment, and the ability to communicate thoughts clearly and simply are essential in this occupation. Decision-making, problem-solving, and research skills also are important. People who choose public relations as a career need an outgoing personality, self-confidence, an understanding of human psychology, and an enthusiasm for motivating people. They should be competitive, yet able to function as part of a team and open to new ideas.

Some organizations, particularly those with large public relations staffs, have formal training programs for new employees. In smaller organizations, new employees work under the guidance of experienced staff members. Beginners often maintain files of material about company activities, scan newspapers and magazines for appropriate articles to clip, and assemble information for speeches and pamphlets. They also may answer calls from the press and the public, work on invitation lists and details for press conferences, or escort visitors and clients. After gaining experience, they write news releases, speeches, and articles for publication or plan and carry out public relations programs. Public relations specialists in smaller firms usually get all-around experience, whereas those in larger firms tend to be more specialized.

The Universal Accreditation Board accredits public relations specialists who are members of the Public Relations Society of America and who participate in the Examination for Accreditation in Public Relations process. This process includes both a readiness review and an examination, which are designed for candidates who have at least 5 years of full-time work or teaching experience in public relations and who have earned a bachelor's degree in a communications-related field.

The readiness review includes a written submission by each candidate, a portfolio review, and dialogue between the candidate and a three-member panel. Candidates who successfully advance through readiness review and pass the computer-based examination earn the Accredited in Public Relations (APR) designation.

The International Association of Business Communicators (IABC) also has an accreditation program for professionals in the communications field, including public relations specialists. Those who meet all the requirements of the program earn the Accredited Business Communicator (ABC) designation. Candidates must have at least 5 years of experience and a bachelor's degree in a communications field and must pass written and oral examinations. They also must submit a portfolio of work samples demonstrating involvement in a range of communications projects and a thorough understanding of communications planning.

Employers may consider professional recognition through accreditation as a sign of competence in this field, which could be especially helpful in a competitive job market.

Promotion to supervisory jobs may come to public relations specialists who show that they can handle more demanding assignments. In public relations firms, a beginner might be hired as a research assistant or account coordinator and be promoted to account executive, senior account executive, account manager, and eventually vice president.

A similar career path is followed in corporate public relations, although the titles may differ. Some experienced public relations specialists start their own consulting firms. (For more information on public relations managers, see the Handbook statement on advertising, marketing, promotions, public relations, and sales managers.)

Public relations specialists held about 188,000 jobs in 2004. Public relations specialists are concentrated in service-providing industries such as advertising and related services; health care and social assistance; educational services; and government. Others worked for communications firms, financial institutions, and government agencies.

Public relations specialists are concentrated in large cities, where press services and other communications facilities are readily available and many businesses and trade associations have their headquarters. Many public relations consulting firms, for example, are in New York, Los Angeles, San Francisco, Chicago, and Washington, DC. There is a trend, however, for public relations jobs to be dispersed throughout the Nation, closer to clients.

Keen competition likely will continue for entry-level public relations jobs, as the number of qualified applicants is expected to exceed the number of job openings. Many people are attracted to this profession because of the high profile nature of the work.

Opportunities should be best for college graduates who combine a degree in journalism, public relations, advertising, or another communications-related field with a public relations internship or other related work experience.

Applicants without the appropriate educational background or work experience will face the toughest obstacles.

Employment of public relations specialists is expected to grow faster than average for all occupations through 2014. The need for good public relations in an increasingly competitive business environment should spur demand for public relations specialists in organizations of all types and sizes.

The value of a company is measured not just by its balance sheet, but also by the strength of its relationships with those on whom it depends for its success. With the increasing demand for corporate accountability, more emphasis will be placed on improving the image of the client, as well as on building public confidence.

Employment in public relations firms should grow as firms hire contractors to provide public relations services rather than support full-time staff. In addition to those arising from employment growth, job opportunities should result from the need to replace public relations specialists who leave the occupation.

Median annual earnings for salaried public relations specialists were $43,830 in May 2004. The middle 50 percent earned between $32,970 and $59,360; the lowest 10 percent earned less than $25,750, and the top 10 percent earned more than $81,120. Median annual earnings in the industries employing the largest numbers of public relations specialists in May 2004 were:

Advertising and related services	$50,450
Management of companies and enterprises	47,330
Business, professional, labour, political, and similar organizations	45,400
Local government	44,550
Colleges, universities, and professional schools	39,610

ADVERTISING, MARKETING, PROMOTIONS, PUBLIC RELATIONS, AND SALES MANAGERS

Significant Points:

- Keen competition for jobs is expected.
- College graduates with related experience, a high level of creativity, strong communication skills, and computer skills should have the best job opportunities.
- High earnings, substantial travel, and long hours, including evenings and weekends, are common.

The objective of any firm is to market and sell its products or services profitably. In small firms, the owner or chief executive officer might assume all advertising, promotions, marketing, sales, and public relations responsibilities. In large firms, which may offer numerous products and services nationally or even worldwide, an executive vice president directs overall advertising, promotions, marketing, sales, and public relations policies. (Executive vice presidents are included in the Handbook statement on top executives.) Advertising, marketing, promotions, public relations, and sales managers coordinate the market research, marketing strategy, sales, advertising, promotion, pricing, product development, and public relations activities.

Advertising managers oversee advertising and promotion staffs, which usually are small, except in the largest firms. In a small firm, managers may serve as liaisons between the firm and the advertising or promotion agency to which many advertising or promotional functions are contracted out. In larger firms, advertising managers oversee in-house account, creative, and media services departments. The account executive manages the account services department, assesses the need for advertising, and, in advertising agencies, maintains the accounts of clients. The creative services department develops the subject matter and presentation of advertising. The creative director oversees the copy chief, art director, and associated staff. The media director oversees planning groups that select the communication media-for example, radio, television, newspapers, magazines, the Internet, or outdoor signs-to disseminate the advertising.

Promotions managers supervise staffs of promotion specialists. These managers direct promotion programs that combine advertising with purchase incentives to increase sales. In an effort to establish closer contact with purchasers-dealers, distributors, or consumers-promotion programs may use direct mail, telemarketing, television or radio advertising, catalogs, exhibits, inserts in newspapers, Internet advertisements or Web sites, in-store displays or product endorsements, and special events. Purchasing incentives may include discounts, samples, gifts, rebates, coupons, sweepstakes, and contests.

Marketing managers develop the firm's marketing strategy in detail. With the help of subordinates, including product development managers and market research managers, they estimate the demand for products and services offered by the firm and its competitors. In addition, they identify potential markets-for example, business firms, wholesalers, retailers, government, or the general public. Marketing managers develop pricing strategy to help firms maximize profits and market share while ensuring that the firm's customers are satisfied. In collaboration with sales, product development, and other managers, they monitor trends that indicate the need for new products and services, and they oversee product development. Marketing managers work with advertising and promotion managers to promote the firm's products and services and to attract potential users.

Public relations managers supervise public relations specialists. (See the Handbook statement on public relations specialists.) These managers direct publicity programs to a targeted audience. They often specialize in a specific area, such as crisis management, or in a specific industry, such as health care. They use every available communication medium to maintain the support of the specific group upon whom their organization's success depends, such as consumers, stockholders, or the general public. For example, public relations managers may clarify or justify the firm's point of view on health or environmental issues to community or special-interest groups.

Public relations managers also evaluate advertising and promotion programs for compatibility with public relations efforts and serve as the eyes and ears of top management. They observe social, economic, and political trends that might ultimately affect the firm, and they make recommendations to enhance the firm's image on the basis of those trends.

Public relations managers may confer with labour relations managers to produce internal company communications-such as newsletters about employee-management relations-and with financial managers to produce company reports. They assist company executives in drafting speeches, arranging interviews, and maintaining other forms of public contact; oversee company archives; and respond to requests for information. In addition, some of these managers handle special events, such as the sponsorship of races, parties introducing new products, or other activities that the firm supports in order to gain public attention through the press without advertising directly.

Sales managers direct the firm's sales program. They assign sales territories, set goals, and establish training programs for the sales representatives. Sales managers advise the sales representatives on ways to improve their sales performance. In large, multiproduct firms, they oversee regional and local sales managers and their staffs. Sales managers maintain contact with dealers and distributors. They analyze sales statistics gathered by their staffs to determine sales potential and inventory requirements and to monitor customers' preferences. Such information is vital in the development of products and the maximization of profits.

Advertising, marketing, promotions, public relations, and sales managers work in offices close to those of top managers. Long hours, including evenings and weekends, are common. In 2004, about two-thirds of advertising, marketing, and public relations managers worked more than 40 hours a week. Working under pressure is unavoidable when schedules change and problems arise, but deadlines and goals must still be met.

Substantial travel may be involved. For example, attendance at meetings sponsored by associations or industries often is mandatory. Sales managers travel to national, regional, and local offices and to the offices of various dealers and distributors. Advertising and promotions managers may travel to meet with clients or representatives of communications media. At times, public relations managers travel to meet with special-interest groups or government officials. Job transfers between headquarters and regional offices are common, particularly among sales managers.

A wide range of educational backgrounds is suitable for entry into advertising, marketing, promotions, public relations, and sales managerial jobs, but many employers prefer those with experience in related occupations plus a broad liberal arts background. A bachelor's degree in sociology, psychology, literature, journalism, or philosophy, among other subjects, is acceptable. However, requirements vary, depending upon the particular job.

For marketing, sales, and promotions management positions, some employers prefer a bachelor's or master's degree in business administration with an emphasis on marketing. Courses in business law, economics, accounting, finance, mathematics, and statistics are advantageous. In highly technical industries, such as computer and electronics manufacturing, a bachelor's degree in engineering or science, combined with a master's degree in business administration, is preferred.

For advertising management positions, some employers prefer a bachelor's degree in advertising or journalism. A course of study should include marketing, consumer behaviour, market research, sales, communication methods and technology, and visual arts-for example, art history and photography.

For public relations management positions, some employers prefer a bachelor's or master's degree in public relations or journalism. The applicant's curriculum should include courses in advertising, business administration, public affairs, public speaking, political science, and creative and technical writing.

For all these specialties, courses in management and the completion of an internship while the candidate is in school are highly recommended. Familiarity with word-processing and database applications also is important for many positions. Computer skills are vital because marketing, product promotion, and advertising on the Internet are increasingly common. Also, the ability to communicate in a foreign language may open up employment opportunities in many rapidly growing areas around the country, especially cities with large Spanish-speaking populations.

Most advertising, marketing, promotions, public relations, and sales management positions are filled by promoting experienced staff or related professional personnel. For example, many managers are former sales representatives, purchasing agents, buyers, or product, advertising, promotions, or public relations specialists. In small firms, where the number of positions is limited, advancement to a management position usually comes slowly. In large firms, promotion may occur more quickly.

Although experience, ability, and leadership are emphasized for promotion, advancement can be accelerated by participation in management training programs conducted by larger firms. Many firms also provide their employees with continuing education opportunities-either in-house or at local colleges and universities-and encourage employee participation in seminars and conferences, often held by professional societies. In collaboration with colleges and universities, numerous marketing and related associations sponsor national or local management training programs. Course subjects include brand and product management, international marketing, sales management evaluation, telemarketing and direct sales, interactive marketing, promotion, marketing communication, market research, organizational communication, and data-processing systems procedures and management. Many firms pay all or part of the cost for employees who successfully complete courses.

Some associations offer certification programs for these managers. Certification-an indication of competence and achievement-is particularly important in a competitive job market. While relatively few advertising, marketing, promotions, public relations, and sales managers currently are certified, the number of managers who seek certification is expected to grow. Today, there are numerous management certification programs based on education and job performance. In addition, The Public Relations Society of America offers a certification program for public relations practitioners based on years of experience and performance on an examination.

Persons interested in becoming advertising, marketing, promotions, public relations, and sales managers should be mature, creative, highly motivated, resistant to stress, flexible, and decisive. The ability to communicate persuasively, both orally and in writing, with other managers, staff, and the public is vital. These managers also need tact, good judgment, and exceptional ability to establish and maintain effective personal relationships with supervisory and professional staff members and client firms.

Because of the importance and high visibility of their jobs, advertising, marketing, promotions, public relations, and sales managers often are prime candidates for advancement to the highest ranks. Well-trained, experienced, and successful managers may be promoted to higher positions in their own or another firm; some become top executives. Managers with extensive experience and sufficient capital may open their own businesses.

Advertising, marketing, promotions, public relations, and sales managers held about 646,000 jobs in 2004. The following tabulation shows the distribution of jobs by occupational specialty:

Sales managers	337,000
Marketing managers	188,000
Advertising and promotions managers	64,000
Public relations managers	58,000

These managers were found in virtually every industry. Sales managers held almost half of the jobs; most were employed in wholesale and retail trade, and finance and insurance industries. Marketing managers held more than fourth of the jobs; the professional, scientific, and technical services industries employed almost one-third of marketing managers. About one-fourth of advertising and promotions managers worked in the professional, scientific, and technical services industries, and the, information industries, including advertising and related services, and publishing industries. Most public relations managers were employed in service-providing industries, such as professional, scientific, and technical services, finance and insurance, health care and social assistance, and educational services.

Advertising, marketing, promotions, public relations, and sales manager jobs are highly coveted and will be sought by other managers or highly experienced professionals, resulting in keen competition. College graduates with related experience, a high level of creativity, and strong communication skills should have the best job opportunities. In particular, employers will seek those who have the computer skills to conduct advertising, marketing, promotions, public relations, and sales activities on the Internet.

Employment of advertising, marketing, promotions, public relations, and sales managers is expected to increase faster than the average for all occupations through 2014, spurred by intense domestic and global competition in products and services offered to consumers. However, projected employment growth varies by industry. For example, employment is projected to grow much faster than average in scientific, professional, and related services, such as computer systems design and related services, and in advertising and related services, as businesses increasingly hire contractors for these services instead of additional full-time staff. By contrast, a decline in employment is expected in many manufacturing industries.

Median annual earnings in May 2004 were $63,610 for advertising and promotions managers, $87,640 for marketing managers, $84,220 sales managers, and $70,000 for public relations managers.

Median annual earnings of advertising and promotions managers in May 2004 in the advertising and related services industry were $89,570.

Median annual earnings in the industries employing the largest numbers of marketing managers in May 2004 were as follows:

Computer systems design and related services	$107,030
Management of companies and enterprises	98,700
Insurance carriers	86,810
Architectural, engineering, and related services	83,610
Depository credit intermediation	76,450

Median annual earnings in the industries employing the largest numbers of sales managers in May 2004 were as follows:

Computer systems design and related services	$119,140
Wholesale electronic markets and agents and brokers	101,930
Automobile dealers	97,460
Management of companies and enterprises	95,410
Machinery, equipment, and supplies merchant wholesalers	84,680

According to a National Association of Colleges and Employers survey, starting salaries for marketing majors graduating in 2005 averaged $33,873; starting salaries for advertising majors averaged $31,340.

Salary levels vary substantially, depending upon the level of managerial responsibility, length of service, education, size of firm, location, and industry. For example, manufacturing firms usually pay these managers higher salaries than do nonmanufacturing firms. For sales managers, the size of their sales territory is another important determinant of salary. Many managers earn bonuses equal to 10 percent or more of their salaries.

Advertising, marketing, promotions, public relations, and sales managers direct the sale of products and services offered by their firms and the communication of information about their firms' activities. Other workers involved with advertising, marketing, promotions, public relations, and sales include actors, producers, and directors; advertising sales agents; artists and related workers; demonstrators, product promoters, and models; market and survey researchers; public relations specialists; sales representatives, wholesale and manufacturing; and writers and editors.

HELPING EXPERT PR RESOURCES AND BUILD NAME RECOGNITION AND SALES

For businesses and organizations that want to harness the power of public relations, we're pleased to offer, through an dynamic company we recently discovered, called "JIAN", a professional caliber software product that provides ready-to-go press release templates for newsworthy events such as a meeting, new company new contract award, new personnel, personnel change, new product, product upgrade, new retail business, new service business, religious group appointment, restaurant opening service program, and sports league. The software also provides worksheets to develop strategic plans, initiatives, and documents, such as case history, company positioning, company spokespeople, product features and benefits, goal setting, media contacts, media calendar, meeting agenda, phone pitch script, pitch letter, PR planning, product positioning, telephone inquiry, and tradshow budget.

If you intend to have a really comprehensive, hard hitting marketing campaign for your company, organization, product, or service, then this software is really a "must have" marketing and planning tool!

POWERFUL AND COST-EFFECTIVE MARKETING TOOLS

An important, but frequently overlooked approach to small business promotion and marketing is public relations. In addition to advertising, sales letters, and face-to-face selling, most well-executed marketing plans include one or more of the following public relations tools: press releases, media interviews, editorials and guest columns (written by you or an associate), seminars and workshops, public speaking engagements, and special events.

A major component of public relations involves "planting" feature stories or news in newspapers, magazines, television or radio programs, and other branches of the media. When a favourable story about your business or organization appears in the press, you not only gain the short-term benefits of the positive publicity, but you can use reprints of the article as a powerful marketing tool. Enclosing a copy of the article with your brochures and sales letters can boost your credibility immeasurably.

Public relations, like other forms of marketing, should not be haphazard or unplanned. Ideally, you should create a 12 month marketing/PR calendar in which you map out the marketing methods you're going to use each month and how your public relations program is going to factor into that strategy. Keep in mind that the more your target audience sees and hears the name of your organization or business, the easier it will be for you and your associates to sell your products, services, or point of view. In conjunction with putting your name out there on a regular basis, here are a few other important principles and ideas to bear in mind as you pursue your public relations and marketing objectives:

* Consider publishing a newsletter for clients, prospects, and the media.
* If you have a new or expanded business, hold a grand opening and invite the media.
* Conduct a press conference if you have something major to unveil or announce.
* Hire a public relations consultant or agency if you need advice or help.
* Take a reporter to lunch (especially if you have a newsworthy story to pitch).
* Be consistent in you message and your image.
* If you're scheduled to be interviewed, anticipate questions and rehearse answers with an associate, friend, or spouse.
* Reinforce your marketing message and positive image in your ads, direct mail campaigns, packaging, sales presentations, speaking engagements, trade shows, press releases, press conferences, and all other contact with the media and the public.
* When you're talking to the media, don't say anything which is "off the record" (it might just end up in print or on the air!).

If you're an authority on your industry or any topic, make that known to the local media. Send them a press packet containing an introductory letter, a studio-quality photo of yourself, a bio, and any appropriate newspaper clippings, brochures, fact sheets, press releases, your business card, resume, and perhaps a page of testimonials or a letter of recommendation(optional), preferably from a community or business leader. It all depends on the situation, your field, and how well established you are. The intention is to have reporters call you for a quote or an interview the next time they do a story on your area of expertise.

Better yet, become proactive and suggest story ideas to news writers and reporters. To increase your effectiveness in "pitching" stories to the media, get to know as many writers and editors, as possible, on a first-name basis.

Becoming known as an authority in your field will call positive attention to you, your business, your organization, or your cause. Not only will that increase your visibility and raise awareness, but it may also result in getting invitations to speak to groups or to conduct workshops. Once your public relations "machine" shifts into high gear, you find yourself achieving more and more success, in terms of generating favourable publicity, enhancing your public image, and attracting customers, clients, members, patients, business associates, or donations, depending on what your objective is.

11

Strategies for Successful Public Relations Marketing

INTRODUCTION

Public Relations involves a variety of programs designed to maintain or enhance a company's image and the products and services it offers. Successful implementation of an effective public relations strategy can be a critical component to a marketing plan.

A public relations (PR) strategy may play a key role in an organization's promotional strategy. A planned approach to leveraging public relations opportunities can be just as important as advertising and sales promotions. Public relations is one of the most effective methods to communicate and relate to the market. It is powerful and, once things are in motion, it is the most cost effective of all promotional activities. In some cases, it is free.

The success of well executed PR plans can be seen through several organizations that have made it a central focus of their promotional strategy. Paul Newman's Salad Dressing, The Body Shop, and Ben & Jerry's Ice Cream have positioned their organizations through effective PR strategies. Intel, Sprint and Microsoft have leveraged public relations to introduce and promote new products and services.

Similar to the foundational goals of marketing, effective public relations seeks to communicate information to:

- Launch new products and services.
- Reposition a product or service.
- Create or increase interest in a product, service, or brand.
- Influence specific target groups.
- Defend products or services that have suffered from negative press or perception.
- Enhance the firm's overall image.
- The result of an effective public relations strategy is to generate additional revenue through greater awareness and information for the products and services an organization offers.

GOALS AND OBJECTIVES

Good strategy begins with identifying your goals and stating your objectives. What are the goals and objectives behind your public relations strategy and can they be measured and quantified?

Each of these areas may reflect the goals your public relations campaign may seek to accomplish.

Press Relations: Communicating news and information of interest about organizations in the most positive light.

Product and Service Promotion: Sponsoring various efforts to publicize specific products or services.

Firm Communications: Promoting a better and more attractive understanding of the organization with internal and external communications.

Lobbying: Communicating with key individuals to positively influence legislation and regulation.

Internal Feedback: Advising decision makers within the organization regarding the public's perception and advising actions to be taken to change negative opinions.

FOREIGN AREA STUDIES

It is commonplace to say that the United States emerged as a world power after the First World War without a base of understanding in its educational and research institutions that was in any way commensurate with its new responsibilities. The American experts at the peace conference performed ably in preparing background papers for the United States delegation, but they were drawn from a very thin layer of scholars available for Such service. What we would now call "European studies" was, of course, relatively well developed, but only with reference to a Europe that extended eastward to the Hohenzollern and Haps burg empires.

Americans fluent in Chinese, Japanese, Arabic, and Turkish, to the very limited extent that they existed, were at this stage much more likely to come from overseas missionary and educational institutions than from American universities. Africa, and South and Southeast Asia, were still well beyond the pale of either academic or political interest. Even as late as the Second World War, there were very few institutions that offered either general courses or specialized education leading to a Ph.D. degree in any of the areas beyond Western Europe.

The Problem

It was as difficult fifty years ago as it is now to write with full assurance as to what Americans at different levels of education and professional specialization should know about overseas countries, which numbered 40 in 1900, 60 in 1920, and about

150 in 1970. Such evaluations depend as much on the changing viewpoints of the social sciences as they do on any fixed structural or functional conceptions.

The academic concern with foreign areas developed in two more or less distinct stages: The first was dominated by the generalist, the "old hand," and the second by the disciplinary specialist. The "old hands" were individuals who had often spent many years in the geographical area of their specialty, and in fact had frequently been born there as children of missionaries, diplomats, educators, archeologists, businessmen, or journalists, and were reasonably fluent in the relevant languages. In addition, they had a strong sense of the history and traditional values of the area, and somewhat less frequently were familiar with its religious and literary heritage. They also knew many of the leading personalities, and at best could talk with authority about current political problems and national aspirations.

The theoretical basis of this approach tended to be in the doctrinaire-liberal tradition: The "old hands" were more likely than not to believe that the political, economic, and social institutions developed in the West European and English-speaking societies were of universal validity and that the main problem of foreign countries was to forget their past and adapt them selves as rapidly as possible to the new, universal pattern. While the members of this "old hand" group that have survived to the present time may now seem out of date, they often had a familiarity with languages and traditions that few can match today.

The second stage of American concern with foreign areas was dominated by the disciplinary specialist. Familiarity with the languages and traditions of foreign areas was now more limited; this was replaced by a professional knowledge of anthropology, economics, geography, history, political science, linguistics, sociology, or social psychology, which made possible a gradual integration of the knowledge about the areas new to American scholarship into the prevalent disciplinary structures of the universities. Western Europe had always formed an integral part of the study of history, literature, political science, and economics, and in some degree served as a model for the newer areas.

To say that most of the relevant disciplines have now turned their attention to foreign areas is, of course, not to say that the right questions are being asked. It is the thesis of this paper that in general the wrong questions have been and are still being asked, and that serious consideration should be given to a new approach to foreign area studies.

Foreign Area Studies Today

An evaluation of foreign area studies in the United States today must take into account the larger body of knowledge known as international studies, of which they form a part together with international relations. Foreign area studies are concerned with the societies of the world, and with such groups of societies as may form geographical regions or areas with common cultural or other characteristics. International relations are concerned with the interactions of individual societies with one another, the legal and organizational frameworks of their relations, and the international system. The comparison of societies and of regional or institutional aspects of societies is usually regarded as a part of foreign area studies, just as the comparison of foreign policies is a part of international relations.

Comparative studies may also be considered a separate field, and indeed the comparative method may be employed in connection with any body of data.

The attention devoted to foreign area studies in the United States has been impressive. Until recent budgetary cuts there were 106 area and language centers, supported in part by the U. S. Office of Education, at 63 colleges and universities, where close to 100 languages were taught. Of these centers, 24 were concerned with Asia, 24 with the USSR and Eastern Europe, 16 with South and Southeast Asia, 16 with Latin America, 13 with Africa, 12 with the Near and Middle East, and one with Northwest Europe.

There were also 21 intensive summer programs offering 36 languages. These programs involved about 60,000 academic-year students, 5,500 summer students, and 2,400 faculty members.

A part of the support for this effort is provided by federal funds administered by the Institute of International Studies of the U.S. Office of Education, under the authority of the National Defense Education Act as amended by the International Education Act of 1966. The annual level of federal support at its height was above $6 million. In addition, Title VI fellowships supported some 2,300 students at a cost of almost $7 million per year. These centers have been concerned primarily with instruction, but at the more advanced level, research has also been involved in the form of the Ph.D. dissertations which for many scholars represent their principal contribution to knowledge.

In addition to these government-sponsored centers, there are many other foreign area programs of various types. There are in addition some 170 coördinating offices for international activities on U.S. campuses, concerned primarily with interdepartmental programs of instruction and related activities. Only exceptionally do they administer research programs. A directory of International Offices on U.S. Campuses (1963) has been prepared by Education and World Affairs, Inc. State governments are also interested in the development of international studies programs in publicly supported educational institutions. In the case of New York, which is no doubt an exception in this as in other respects, the International Studies Center of the State University of New York administers the integration of international studies and world affairs programs on 60 campuses. The State University also maintains a Center for International Programs and Services, which distributes foreign area materials and also organizes conferences and research programs.

In the federal government there are no fewer than 159 programs in 31 agencies that deal with education and research activities concerning foreign areas, either in the United States or in coöperation with foreign governments. In the more limited area of cultural exchanges, the Inventory of Federal

Programs Involving Educational Activities Concerned With Improving International Understanding and Coöperation (Office of Education, Department of Health, Education, and Welfare [HEW] 1969) describes federal activities in this field.

These activities are coördinated to some extent by tbe Inter Agency Council on International Education and Cultural Affairs, headed by the Assistant Secretary for Education and Cultural Affairs of the Department of State, and the Federal Inter Agency Council on Education, headed by the Assistant Secretary for Education, HEW. There has nonetheless been criticism in Congress of the diversity and lack of coördinated direction of these numerous programs, and the Appropriations Act for Fiscal Year 1968 directed the Secretary of Health, Education, and Welfare to conduct a study "with the objective of determining the extent of adjustment and consolidation of these programs that is desirable in order that their objectives may be more efficiently and expeditiously accomplished...." Such a study was prepared by Education and World Affairs in 1969, entitled Directions for the Future: Federal Programs in Education Designed to In fluence International Understanding and Coöperation.

In the area of research, as distinguished from the wide variety of international, educational, and cultural activities in which the federal government is involved, an important effort at coördination is made by the Foreign Area Research Coördination Group (FAR), under the auspices of the Office of External Research, Department of State. The federal agencies engaged in research or support of research are all represented on FAR, which also seeks to keep in touch with academic research. FAR publishes a bi-monthly newsletter, FAR Horizons, which contains information about institutions and projects in the field of international studies. It supports the FAR Documentation Center, which collects papers prepared for academic and professional meetings, and other recently completed unpublished studies. A list of these papers is issued periodically. This office also published Foreign Affairs Research: A Directory of Government Resources (1967).

It is not easy to evaluate such a large and complex enterprise and to distinguish foreign area studies from other aspects of international studies. One may nevertheless make a few general comments which will serve to measure the achievements of the past generation and at the same time to indicate what remains to be done before our understanding of the societies of the world will be adequate to the tasks that face us.

TRAINING OF SPECIALISTS

As regards instruction in foreign areas and languages at the undergraduate and graduate levels, the objective is to meet the needs of faculties in educational institutions, and to provide area and language specialists for public service, business, and the professions. This need varies, depending on the relative importance of the various foreign areas to the United States from a cultural and political standpoint, and there is no adequate way of measuring how many foreign area specialists are needed in the United States. One may nevertheless hazard a guess that only as regards Western Europe, Russia, Japan, and possibly the Arabic countries, does the number of people being trained even begin to meet the current need. Moreover, there are wide discrepancies between disciplines, in some of which few, if any, area specialists are being trained. As for other world areas, the number being educated falls very far short of what may be considered adequate to meet national requirements.

More important than the number and distribution by area of the specialists being trained is the substance of the education that is offered. This leads directly to the question of what we know about foreign areas--for what is taught is, by and large, what we think we know, assuming the normal lag between the advance of research and its dissemination in educational institutions. This is the essential link between research and instruction, and it is difficult to separate the research that generates our knowledge of foreign areas from the teaching of this knowledge in educational institutions. These are two aspects of the same subject. They can be separated from a budgetary and from a logical standpoint, but what we say about one aspect largely applies to the other as well.

The principal shortcoming of American research on foreign areas may be due to the fact that it has been based primarily on a comparison between these areas and societies, and the United States. This basis of comparison has more often been implicit than explicit, and it stems from the natural initial question: How do these foreign societies differ from ours? This method of proceeding from the known to the unknown produces the fundamental methodological defect of judging foreign areas by American or "Western" standards. This ethnocentric bias is frequently set in undergraduate courses on "Western Civilization," which describe modern history in terms of the worldwide expansion of the values and institutions of the West European and English-speaking societies. Most of our research and writing on foreign areas has not departed significantly from this pattern.

It has generally been assumed that the natural course of political development under the impact of industrialization is the growth of a multiparty political system of representative government. In countries as different as Russia, Turkey, Egypt, and China, it has been assumed that leaders advocating a "Western" model would emerge in due course, and that they have been delayed or obstructed either by unusually stubborn traditional systems or by radical dictators employing illegitimate force. It was not until the 1950's, for example, that Kemal Ataturk came to be appreciated not simply as "another dictator" like Musso lini, Stalin, Hitler, and Franco, but as a modernizing leader whose creative ideas contributed to the development of a country which had no tradition of multiparty government. It was not until the 1960's that political scientists could discuss without embarrassment the relative advantages of military leaders and one-party political systems.

Of the many factors entering into this culture-bound approach of American scholarship to foreign areas, two may be singled out as critical. One has been the paradigm represented by the French Revolution. It has long been a matter of faith that old regimes give way to middle-class systems, which in turn develop into multiparty representative political systems. American scholars were not alone, of course, in reflecting this point of view, but it appears to have been a particularly influential interpretation in this country. In due course the Marxists and Marxist-Leninists added a new dimension to this approach by maintaining that a middle-class system would in turn be followed by a proletarian system, but this view did not have any great impact on American scholarship. These two views, which may be called doctrinaire-liberal and Marxist-Leninist, equally ethnocentric in their different ways, have coexisted without having much impact on each other.

A second factor that has tended to strengthen this ethnocentric bias is the idea that form follows function. It is maintained that since in the West-European and English-speaking societies the older feudal institutions were transformed into the political, economic, and social forms that we fondly characterize as "Western," therefore these must be the characteristic institutional forms of the functions performed by all societies as they are transformed by modern knowledge. In this view, the "Western" forms--political, economic, and social institutions--must be as universally valid as the modern knowledge which they reflect.

A NEW APPROACH

How can we get away from this inherent ethnocentric bias and seek an approach to the study of foreign societies that relies on universal criteria that are free, as much as possible, from the model represented by our own society? The approach proposed here is one that interprets the development of contemporary societies in terms of interactions between the diverse traditional institutions of each society and the common features of change that, for want of a better term, one may call "modernity." One may then go on to discuss the specific aspects of modernity that seem to be most suitable as a means of understanding current trends in the modern world.

An approach that is generalized to this extent will embrace developments not only in foreign areas but in the United States as well. It will seek to do justice to the diversity among and within the approximately 150 or more politically distinct societies of the world, as well as to the common characteristics that they will increasingly share as they succeed in applying the results of modern knowledge.

The first step in understanding a modern society is to understand the heritage of traditional institutions as they existed in a relatively stable form on the eve of the impact of modern knowledge. This relatively stable traditional, or premodern, period is different for each society. It ranges from feudalism in the case of the West European societies, to the Muscovite and Tokugawa periods in the case of Russia and Japan, to the colonial periods lasting into the mid-twentieth century in the cases of the newer states. The existence of such traditional periods can scarcely be questioned, although there is, of course, plenty of room for argument regarding their chronological limits and their precise characteristics.

What is significant in understanding foreign areas today is the diversity of the traditional institutional heritages of each society. These traditional institutions are diverse not only in their intellectual, political, economic, and social forms, but also in their adaptability to modern functions. Some traditional institutions--the caste system in India, the formidable ethnocentrism of China, the institution of slavery in the United States and else where--represent major obstacles to modernization. In other cases--the elements of political representation in feudalism, the relatively well-organized governmental institutions of Oriental despotisms, the proclivity of Russian and Japanese societies to ward adapting foreign institutions to their own use, the adaptability of the societies of the new world were settled by modern-minded immigrants (United States, Canada, Australia, and New Zealand)--relatively modest changes are called for by the transitions from tradition to modernity.

Form thus follows function only in a very abstract sense. In practice, some traditional forms may be destroyed by modernity, while others adapt rather easily. In this adaptation to a modern environment, some institutions disappear, while others are still recognizable after a century or more of rapid change.

In England, for example, agricultural production and medicine have changed much more since the seventeenth century than Parliament or the English language. A relatively modern society is not totally different from a traditional society, but is rather (from a traditional viewpoint) a distorted version of it--a distortion due to varying degrees and types of adaptation. Since no two traditional societies are quite alike, and no two adapt in quite the same way, no two relatively modern societies are quite alike either. This fundamental diversity of relatively modern societies should be a basic concept in any understanding of foreign areas.

The second main element of modernization is represented by the functional consequences of modernity. The characteristic of modernity that requires traditional institutions to change their ways is basically the "knowledge explosion." Nothing has changed fundamentally in historical times except our knowledge of the world. The material basis of everything we do today, including sending people around the moon, was available 5,000 years ago. The only thing that was lacking was the knowledge of how to use the available materials.

It is the central nervous systems of individuals operating on the environment, thinking about the environment, finding out new things about it, and interacting with one another, that accounts for change. Important changes in climate, in geography, and also in the capacities of man occurred in earlier periods, but in historical times the only change has been the change in our knowledge of the world around us. This was relatively stable for several thousand years before modern times, and the level of knowledge of the world prevalent in Western Europe in the Middle Ages did not differ greatly from that of the ancient Greeks and Romans. In contrast to the relative stability of knowledge for several thousand years before modern times, a knowledge explosion has occurred since the seventeenth century in the course of which the application of the scientific method has led to sweeping changes in all realms of human activity.

From an intellectual standpoint, the modern era is characterized by the advancement of knowledge in all spheres. It is still advancing very rapidly, and about 20 percent of our Gross National Product (GNP) is now devoted to knowledge in all its forms. Its most obvious form is technology, leading to the industrialization of the modern world.

The main political consequence of modernization is the consolidation of decision-making, and, in effect, an increase in the authority of central governments. Traditional political systems have adapted to this change in various ways. Feudal systems have generally developed into representative governments; others with traditionally autocratic institutions have become totalitarian; and yet others have sought to borrow modern political forms rather than develop their own. This has very little to do with the ideologies of socialism and capitalism, and, in fact, both the Soviet Union and the United States expend about the same proportion of their GNP on government. All modern governments have to perform certain functions, regardless of their ideology, simply because industrialized and urbanized societies are integrated and mobilized to such an extent that society-wide administrative functions are inevitably strengthened.

In the economic sphere, the main functional consequence of the knowledge explosion is, of course, economic growth resulting from the mechanization of production. There has been a very fundamental transformation from the simple agricultural procedures of traditional societies to the industrialization of all aspects of production that is possible today. This transformation has been so dramatic that industrialization is frequently equated with modernization, although, in fact, it is only one of several constituent elements.

From a social standpoint, modernization has meant the transformation of the way people live and earn their living. In traditional societies, 80 to 90 percent of the population is engaged in a rural way of life, whereas after modernization a similar proportion is engaged in industry, the professions, and service occupations. Changes in family structure and educational opportunities are other functional consequences of this knowledge explosion. Individual psychology is also transformed, since a different personality is required for successful survival in the modern world than one that is adapted to a village environment.

EFFECTS OF MODERNIZATION ON SOCIETY

These functional consequences of modernity are the same for all countries. The functions that societies must be able to perform as they adapt their institutions to the consequences of modern life are the same around the world, but the base from which change takes place is different in each of the approximately 150 independent countries, as well as some thirty or forty dependent territories that are still lined up waiting to be born as independent states. All face common problems, but they face them in different ways because they start out with different institutions.

12

Press Release: A Case Study

INTRODUCTION

The mid-1970s is often remembered as the "golden era" of American journalism. Most famously, the media exposed the crimes of the Nixon White House, reducing a president who had won re-election by a landslide two years before to a national laughingstock who resigned in disgrace before he was impeached.

But Watergate was only one among many scandals during this period. Some of the darkest secrets of how government and business actually function in a supposedly democratic system were laid bare by a seemingly emboldened press.

So it might come as a surprise to learn that Katharine Graham, publisher of the Washington Post, which led the way in exposing Watergate, was less than pleased. A few weeks after Nixon resigned in 1974, Graham lectured a meeting of media executives that the press should "be rather careful about its role. We may have acquired some tendencies about over-involvement that we had overcome."

Three decades later, no one could describe the mainstream media as "over-involved"--unless they meant "over-involved" in presenting the undiluted propaganda of the powers that be.

End Times: The Death of the Fourth Estate, a new book by CounterPunch editors Alexander Cockburn and Jeffrey St. Clair, documents the current dismal state of the media-

-from the "embedded" reporters who present the Pentagon's line, to a punditocracy that cheerleads for war, to the editors and executives who oversee a press characterized by a mind-numbing conformity.

Why are the media so tame?

After all, the government doesn't censor them to get the stories it wants.

End Times documents some examples of outright pressure applied against an unwilling press. But these are the exceptions. As a rule, the U.S. political establishment can count on the media taming itself--acting like "the really well-trained dog," in the words of George Orwell, "that turns somersaults when there is no whip."

As Cockburn writes in an article dissecting the New York Times under former Executive Editor A.M. Rosenthal, "[M]ostly, supervision is not such an explicit process. Every reporter and editor in the news business has a compass in their heads which alerts them within the fraction of a degree to the prejudices and preferences of the boss, whether it's Katharine Graham, or Ben Bradlee, or Rosenthal or Murdoch or the Executive Network News Producer or whoever is construed as ruling the roost."

Journalists at major media outlets learn what is expected of them, and those who want to advance--and most do--adapt themselves to the agenda, spoken or not, of their employers, as well as the people and institutions they report on.

As Charles Lewis, a former 60 Minutes producer who resigned to form the Center for Public Integrity, put it, "The values of the news media are the same as those of the elite, and they badly want to be viewed by the elites as acceptable. Socially, culturally and economically, they belong to the group of people who they are covering."

Ben Bradlee, the editor of the Post during Watergate, confirms Lewis' observation. "Reporters are more conservative than the previous generation," he said. "And I think there's a very good reason for that. They get paid a hell of a lot better. It's hard to be conservative on $75 a week, but seventy-five grad, you begin to think of the kids and the bank account and the IRA and roll it over and all this stuff."

In his essay titled "The Fall of the Washington Post," CounterPunch contributor Ken Silverstein provides the final proof by citing the quintessential celebrity journalist Diane Sawyer.

"During an episode on social spending, Sawyer berated a welfare mother who was illegally working two part-time jobs in order to supplement her $600 per month welfare benefits," Silverstein writes.

"'You know, people say you should not have children if you can't support them,' Sawyer sternly lectured her victim. As pointed out by FAIR, the media watchdog group, Sawyer earns every day almost as much as the welfare mom earned per year: $16,700."

These are the people who determine what's news, and therefore it's no surprise that the media tend--in contrast to the right wing's claims about liberal bias--to reinforce existing prejudice, rather than challenge it in any significant way.

Thus, one section of End Times is devoted to describing how the supposedly liberal media continue to peddle racism, in a variety of forms.

In an article about Gary Webb--the San Jose Mercury News reporter pilloried by his media "colleagues" for his articles revealing a link between the CIA, the U.S.-backed contra army that fought the left-wing Nicaraguan government in the 1980s, and the epidemic of crack cocaine in Black Los Angeles--Cockburn and St. Clair highlight how African Americans were chastised for their "paranoia" in believing Webb's story.

Blacks, the two write, "get it coming and going. Terrible things happen to them, and then they're patronized in the

Washington Post for imagining that such terrible things might happen again."

A media intent on reinforcing conventional wisdom is all the more susceptible to the professional hucksters--otherwise known as public relations consultants--whose job is to sell the story or image that their bosses want to see in the press.

St. Clair's article "How to Sell a War" takes a look at the Bush administration's sales force for the Iraq war, whose mission was to underline and reinforce the doctrines of the administration's neocons to an accommodating media.

"Facts," St. Clair writes, "were never important to the Bush team. They were disposable nuggets that could be discarded at will and replaced by whatever new rationale that played favourably with their polls and focus groups."

This statement of the central rule of perception-making under Bush Jr. is echoed in Cockburn's gleeful obituary to "The Great Communicator," Ronald Reagan. "Truth, for him," Cockburn writes, "was what he happened to be saying at the time. He went one better than George Washington, in that he couldn't tell a lie, and he couldn't tell the truth, since he couldn't tell the difference between the two."

Reagan's still hallowed image depended on what Cockburn calls the "news spasms" manufactured by his handlers to create "a national mood of consensus," with Reagan as the placid, grandfatherly master of ceremonies.

In reality, Cockburn writes, Reagan was "a vicious man, with a breezy indifference to suffering and the consequences of decision...[for which] Dante would surely have consigned him to one of the lowest circles of hell, to roast for all eternity in front of a malfunctioning TV set and a dinner tray swinging out of reach like the elusive fruits that tortured Tantalus."

Amid this otherwise grim picture, Cockburn and St. Clair present a reason to be cheerful. In the book's introduction, they write, "[T]he old David vs. Goliath struggle of the left pamphleteers battling the vast print combines of the news barons has equaled up," thanks to the Internet.

CounterPunch's Web site has at least 100,000 visitors a day, they point out. "Thirty years ago, many of these pieces, challenging the official nonsense peddled in the mass-market media, would have been doomed to small-circulation magazines, or a 30-second précis on Pacifica radio...Not any more. We can get a news story from a CounterPuncher in Gaza or Ramallah or Oaxaca or Vidharba, and have it out to a world audience in a matter of hours."

This is food for thought. The Internet has made it much easier to get access to the real story, buried under the myths and bromides of the U.S. media. If the politicians and pundits complain that official Washington has become a place of nonstop scandal, it's partly because it's harder in the era of the Internet to keep a secret from those who want to find it out.

But this point does raise another question. In spite of this unprecedented access to information, the U.S. government was still able to get away with its invasion of Iraq. The facts to debunk the lies that justified the invasion could be found easily--on CounterPunch, in Socialist Worker and well beyond. But that didn't stop it from happening.

To successfully challenge wars and injustice, more than the right information is needed. The facts and ideas put forward in books like End Times, on Web sites like CounterPunch and in publications like Socialist Worker need to be put into practice--by activists who share both the bitter anger of this book toward the everyday crimes of the system and the hope that struggle can win genuine change.

ENGLISH LANGUAGE REQUIREMENT FOR FDA DOCUMENTS

Definition: The term document applies to official records which are considered to be U.S. Government property regardless of the media e.g. Regulatory notes (electronic and hardcopy), memoranda, inspection reports, e-mails, and official government forms (e.g. SF-71, FDA-482, FDA-483, etc.)

All official FDA documents generated during the routine duties shall be completed in English. This requirement is necessary to facilitate efficiency in the workplace. For instance, many of your work products used in support of FDA's regulatory process are subject to review and auditing by your supervisor, utilized by your co-workers, and others, including the public, in that they are releasable under the Freedom of Information Act (FOIA). The Agency does not have the resources to assure the accurate and timely English translation of documents written in a non English language in order to facilitate their use in the conduct of official business. English is generally considered to be the common language of the U.S., therefore it is necessary to standardize the language utilized in the production of official FDA documents.

Additionally, FDA imposes English only requirements on the public for information submitted to the Agency. For example 21 Code of Federal Regulations section 803.13(a) (English Reporting Requirement) states that " All reports required in this part which are submitted in writing or electronic equivalent shall be submitted to FDA in English."

TRAVEL

All official travel must be authorized and approved with a valid travel order (T.O.) using FDA's on-line travel management program GovTrip. Emergency travel can be approved and the travel order prepared and authorized after the fact. "After the fact" T.O.s should be utilized on a very limited basis.

The federal travel regulations contained in 41 CFR 301, Department of Health and Human Services (DHHS) Travel

Manual, and the Food and Drug Administration (FDA) supplements thereto, govern official travel. Become familiar with these documents. All material contained in the Investigations Operations Manual (IOM) must be used in conjunction with, and subject to, federal travel regulations. Additional travel information can be obtained from the Office of Financial Management (OFM) Intranet home page: http://intranet.fda.gov/ofm/default.htm.

For foreign travel, be aware that there are differences in reporting requirements and reimbursable expenses. See the Guide to International Inspections and Travel, Chapter 1, Subchapter 110-Travel, for specifics.

Effective March 1, 2000, federal employees must put most official travel-related charges on government-issued credit cards, with exceptions only for expenses that are either relatively minor or inconvenient for credit card usage such as parking, local transportation, tips, phone calls, and certain expenses for which credit cards are not accepted.

FDA selected Northrop Grumman's GovTrip as their E-Government Travel Service. GovTrip is accessed at www.govtrip.com. GovTrip will enable FDA travelers and travel preparers to make travel reservations, book hotel accommodations and rental car reservations, and create authorizations and vouchers (including local travel vouchers) in a single web-based system. In addition, GovTrip will interface with the Unified Financial Management System (UFMS) for obligation and payment of travel vouchers. Payments will include direct payment to US Bank for expenses charged to the individual's official government travel credit card. The system incorporates Federal Government travel policies which include the city pair airfare contract program and Federal Travel Regulations and is structured to require justification if you want to deviate from General Services Administration's (GSA) regulations. A policy has been established with the FDA so that your government-issued credit card will be your primary method of billing and payment when you book flights, make hotel reservations, or reserve a rental car. Additional information can be obtained by contacting your Administrative Officer (AO) or visiting OFM's website: http://intranet.fda.gov/ofm/default.htm.

COMMON CARRIER

Request round-trip tickets when it can be expected you will use them. This reduces paperwork costs, even though there may be no savings on the tickets themselves. You should cancel reserved tickets if you will not be using them. Failure to do so may result in charges levied by the carrier. Note the date and time of your cancellation, and the name or code number of the agent that you advised. Unused tickets must be returned to your AO or Travel Management Center.

Requirements which authorize you to use cash payments for procurement of common carrier transportation and related expenses, in lieu of your government-issued credit card, or centrally billed account, are specified in 41 CFR 301-72.200 and 301-51.100. Cash payments are generally permitted:

1. To obtain passenger transportation services, in an emergency, for any amount when authorized by your District Director (DD) and documented on your T.O. Otherwise, cash and personal credit cards may not be used for transportation expenses exceeding $100.00.
2. To pay air excess baggage charges up to $15.00 for each leg of a trip.

When cash is used, claim a reimbursement on your travel voucher and submit your ticket stubs or other appropriate receipts. You must also explain the circumstances for using cash on your travel voucher. See IOM 1.2.7 for mandatory statements required on a travel voucher.

Air

It is FDA's policy to require all travelers to use coach class service for official travel. A contract air carrier must be used unless one of three approved exceptions is met and your District Director approves another carrier. See your fiscal clerk for further information. Justification for use of non-contract carriers must be approved on the Travel Order by the Regional Food and Drug Director (RFDD), DD or Administrative Officer, or on the voucher, if "after the fact." Refer to Federal Travel Regulation (FTR) 301-10.107 and 301-10.108 for the mandatory use of a contract city-pair fare.

Exceptions to using City Pair Program are:

1. Contract service is not available in time to accomplish the purpose of your travel
2. Use of contract service would require you to incur unnecessary overnight lodging costs that would increase the total cost of the trip
3. Contract service is outside normal working hours
4. A non-contract carrier offers a lower fare (available to the general public), the use of which will result in a lower total trip cost to the Government
5. Cost effective rail service is available and is consistent with mission requirements

The Associate Commissioner for Management must authorize First Class travel. The use of first class travel must be pre-approved, and such approval will not be granted, even for medical reasons, unless business class is not available.

The National Defense Authorization Act for Fiscal Year 2002, Section 1116 specifically states that federal employees may retain for personal use promotion items, including frequent flyer miles, earned on official travel. Normally it is the policy of the Government that employees generally must travel by coach class accommodations. However, you may upgrade your transportation class to premium service e.g. business class/first-class with your personal funds or your frequent flyer miles based on regulations found in FTR

301-10.123 and 301-10.124. Accommodations other than coach will be approved if in met in accordance with the FTR and the NTEU-MOU for foreign inspections.

Consistent with FTR 301-12.2, you may be reimbursed expenses related to baggage, but you should be prudent and only request reimbursement for reasonable excess baggage authorized and approved in advance on the travel order.

Auto Rental

GSA and the Department of Defense (DOD) both provide employees with a nationwide commercial auto rental program. The Federal Travel Directory, published monthly on floppy diskette, contains a list of vehicle leasing companies participating in this program. Agency policy dictates leasing the least expensive auto to satisfy the transportation requirements.

Commercial auto rental is available when specifically authorized by a special or blanket T.O. You will be reimbursed for rental expense when it is properly vouchered and your receipt is attached to your travel voucher.

Optional Collision Damage Insurance known as CDW will not be reimbursed. Participating rental companies have agreed to settle any claim for damages with the FDA. It is important to note that only damages incident to official travel will be covered by this agreement. If an investigation shows your vehicle damage or personal injury was the result of your unauthorized use of a rental vehicle, you may be personally liable for all related costs.

CDW is required for foreign travel and will be reimbursed. See the Guide to International Inspections and Travel, 211.7-Auto Rental.

Travelers are required to adhere to the same rules and regulations covering government owned vehicles when using a rental car while on official business.

Taxi

Reimbursement for the use of taxicabs will only be allowed when authorized on your T.O. Allowable tips are 15% of the reimbursable fare. Receipts are required for fares over $75.00.

You will be reimbursed for the usual cab and/or airport limousine fares plus tip from your home/office to the common carrier terminal on the day you depart on an official overnight trip, and upon your return. In lieu of cab, you may use your personal car at a mileage rate not to exceed the cab fare plus tip. See your administrative personnel for current mileage rates, the maximum allowable taxicab fares, and other pertinent details.

Accident Insurance

The government will not pay or reimburse you if you purchase accident insurance. Obtaining accident insurance is at your expense since you are covered while on official business by workmen''s compensation insurance.

Many insurance policies will not cover you if you perform any duties connected with your job while on an interstate transportation carrier. This could affect you if you perform on-board inspections under the Interstate Travel Sanitation Program during a trip.

Gainsharing

The Government Employees Incentive Awards Act, 5 USC Paragraphs 4501-4507, authorizes an agency to pay a cash award for "efficiency" or "economy". FDA in conjunction with the National Treasury Employees Union (NTEU) implemented a Gainsharing Travel Savings Program which rewards you if you save the FDA money while you are on temporary travel (TDY). Your participation is optional. The Agency''s gainsharing policy as well as filing instructions for gainsharing claims can be found by accessing OFM''s website: http://intranet.fda.gov/ofm/travel/authorization/gainsharing/default.htm.

Government Furnished Vehicles (GFVs)

GFVs are provided for official purposes only. The term "official purpose" shall be interpreted strictly, and not construed to mean mingling of official business with non-official business. Using a GFV for sightseeing, personal business, personal convenience or preference will be construed as unauthorized use of a GFV. The distance involved in any such misuse is irrelevant. The following is an excerpt from the DHHS Travel Manual Appendix A 1-2.6a., dated May 31, 1988 which further defines official purpose:

"Use of Government-furnished Vehicles."

a. "Use limited to official purposes-When a Government furnished vehicle is used by an employee for official travel, its use shall be limited to official purposes (31 U.S.C. 638a) which include transportation between places where the employee's presence is required incident to official business; between such places and places of temporary lodging when public transportation is unavailable or its use is impractical; and between either of the above places and suitable eating places, drug stores, barber shops, places of worship, cleaning establishments, and similar places necessary for the sustenance, comfort, or health of the employee in order to foster the continued efficient performance of Government business." You are responsible at all times for the proper care, operation, maintenance, and protection of a GFV. If you willfully or knowingly use or authorize the use of a GFV for other than official purposes, you are subject to suspension or removal.

Interagency Motor Pool

GFVs for district operations are furnished by the regional GSA motor pool. Be guided by the district operating procedures in effect for the appropriate regional pool.

Vehicle Operation-You are required to have a valid state, District of Columbia, or commonwealth operator's permit for the type vehicle to be operated, and a valid DHHS identification document (i.e. Agency ID card, credentials, building pass, etc.).

Each district has working arrangements for the repair and maintenance of vehicles, either with GSA contractors or the GSA motor pool. It is your responsibility to adhere to those safety and maintenance checks. Do not operate cars known to be mechanically unsafe. Handle emergency repairs in travel status in accordance with your District and GSA motor pool procedures.

Purchase gas and oil for your GFV with GSA Credit Cards. Make emergency purchases with cash only when the GSA Credit Card is refused. Your receipts are required by the GSA motor pool. Provide for the safe and proper overnight storage of GFVs while you are in travel status, and put the charges on your travel voucher. You are responsible for all traffic violations, including parking fines, you incur during the use and operation of a GFV. See DHHS Material Management Manual Section 103-38-052.1.

Allowance-While on official business, you may be reimbursed for parking fees or overnight storage charges. Put these charges on your travel voucher. Receipts are required when available.

Bridge, ferry and road tolls may be paid in cash. Put these charges on your travel voucher. Receipts are only required for amounts over $75.00.

Accidents

Immediate Action-Render first aid. If you are injured, obtain emergency treatment. Contact police.

Information to be Obtained

Information to be obtained:

1. Description of vehicles involved, including license numbers

2. Name, address and other pertinent information about drivers and owners of other vehicles; exchange state driver license information if possible
3. Names, addresses and signed statements of witnesses
4. Names, official affiliation of investigating police officers
5. Photographs of the scene and the damage
6. Make no statements as to responsibility for the accident, except to your supervisor or investigating official.

Reporting

Report the accident to the police after rendering emergency first aid to the injured. Telephone your supervisor and the chief of the motor pool from which the vehicle is assigned, unless your supervisor advises you the district will handle it.

1. Complete the following forms and submit as required:
    1. "Motor Vehicle Accident Report" (SF-91)
    2. Copy of an traffic regulations or ordinance which was violated
    3. Results of any trial or disposition of summons if any arrests were made or charges preferred.
    4. "Claim for Damage, Injury or Death" (SF-95) or other written notification of an incident accompanied by a claim. (SF-95 or statement constituting a claim must be date-stamped by the office initially receiving the claim to document the exact date the claim was received.) To be completed by claimant/non-government employee.
    5. Investigation Reports and Policy Reports
    6. Statement of Witness (SF-94)
    7. Itemized receipt of payment for necessary repairs or two itemized written estimates of cost of repairs

8. Statement listing date of purchase, purchase price and salvage value where repair is not economical
9. Photographs of damage and/or scene of accident if available

2. File reports to comply with all local and state laws dealing with accident reporting. Keep copies of all reports made and attach them to the federal accident report.
3. Check with your personal insurance carrier for their requirements.
4. Immediately submit to your supervisor any notice, summons, legal paper or claim, which may subsequently arise from the accident.
5. Check with your district safety officer to determine if additional reports or information are needed.

Liability

The Federal Drivers Act (28 U.S.C. 2679(a)-(e)) was enacted to protect government drivers from personal liability while driving within the scope of their employment. This means you must be on official business to be covered. It relieves you from the burden of acquiring private automobile liability insurance for driving while on the job.

The government"s exclusive liability provided by this Act is predicated on its status as employer, without regard to whether the vehicle involved is government owned or privately owned.

The Military Personnel and Civilian Employees" Claim Act of 1964 allows for claims against FDA by employees, provided the loss or damage was within the scope of their employment and the employee (claimant) is free of negligence regarding those losses (See IOM 1.2.2.3.1). The Federal Tort Claims Act provides for claims generally coming from outside the Agency where the activities of the agency, or specific individual employees are negligent and cause death, injuries, or property loss or damage (See IOM 1.2.2.3.2).

Claims should be submitted through your Administrative Office to the Office of Shared Services, Fleet Manager, HFA-720, 12345 Parklawn Drive, Rockville, MD 20857. The claim will be reviewed and forwarded to Program Support Center (PSC) for processing.

Military Personnel and Civilian Employees' Claim Act of 1964

Documentation and information to be submitted as follows for military personnel and civilian employees" claims under the Military Personnel and Civilian Employees" Claim Act of 1964.

Claims Involving Household Moves:

1. "Employee Claim for Loss or Damage to Personal Property" (HHS-481)
2. Schedule of Property
3. Household Inventory showing items claims
4. Other documents that may provide evidence of damage or loss
5. Proof of Ownership
6. Cost of Repair (if damage is over $50.00 submit receipt of cost of repair or estimate of cost on company letterhead)
7. Photographs if available
8. Copies of private claims if applicable (claims must be filed seeking recovery from carrier before FDA claim can be filed.)

Claims Involving Property Loss or Damage:

1. "Employee Claim for Loss or Damage to Personal Property" (HHS-481)

2. Schedule of Property
3. Proof of Ownership
4. Cost of Repair (if damage is over $50.00 submit a receipt for the cost of repair or estimate of cost on company letterhead)
5. Photographs if available
6. Copies of private claims if applicable
7. Police report and/or other agency report and witness statements if appropriate

Motor Vehicle Accidents-See IOM 1.2.2.2

Use of a GFV between Residence and Place of Employment

Use of government owned or leased autos between your residence and place of employment is approved by the Secretary, DHHS, for certain job series as stated in FDA Staff Manual Guide (SMG) 2173.1.

The use of a DHHS-16 "Request To Use Government Furnished Vehicle For Transportation Between Domicile and Place of Employment" is no longer required, however, local management may continue to use the form or establish a verbal approval process, if desired. The Daily Log of Government Vehicle (Form FDA-3369) must be maintained by all approved persons using a GFV, assuring that all items indicated on the form are completed for each trip.

The DHHS now requires that each person taking a GFV home, in order to perform field work, must indicate in Column 10 on the Form 3369, the location of their residence. The Daily Log must be kept for at least a period of three years and must be available for audit purposes.

The use of Form DHHS-17 "Quarterly Report on Use of Government-Owned or Leased Vehicles Between Domicile and Place of Employment" is no longer required.

Per Diem and Subsistence

Subsistence is the cost of lodging, meals, tips, and the miscellaneous expenses you incur while in travel status. Per Diem is based on the actual cost of lodging, plus a set amount for "Meals and Incidental Expenses" (M&IE), not to exceed the maximum rate for the prescribed city or area.

Note: For domestic travel only, report lodging taxes separate from lodging expenses and claim them in the "Other" column on your travel voucher. Foreign travel taxes still remain a part of your lodging expenses.

Lodging expenses should be paid using your government-issued credit card, when possible. The credit card bill will be mailed directly to you. It is your responsibility to pay the bill on time. The FDA will reimburse late charges on your bill only when you can show the late payment was due to late reimbursement of funds by the FDA.

Accurately record all of your expenditures. Document the date of your departure from each point where your duty is performed. Be guided by your district"s policy for where to record this information, e.g. in an administrative diary, etc.

Administrative Notes-Your regulatory notes should not contain notes of a purely administrative nature (documentation of travel, expenses [tolls, sample costs, etc.], fiscal data, mileage, etc.) These administrative notes can be documented in some kind of an administrative diary. They do not need to be kept in a permanent record other than the completed Travel Voucher, Claim for Reimbursement for Expenditures on Official Business, Receipt for Samples, etc. Follow your district"s requirements for maintaining this information.

Per Diem Rates

Per Diem commences when you depart your home, office, or other point of departure, and terminates when you return to your home, office, or other point. This applies whether you are traveling by auto or by common carrier.

The M&IE Allowance is 3/4 of the daily rate on the first and last day of travel when overnight travel is involved, and the full daily rate for each intervening day. M&IE may apply where there is no overnight lodging. However, M&IE will not be allowed for periods of time less than twelve hours.

Your work time plus your total commute time must be greater than twelve hours for you to be eligible for M&IE.

Change of Official Station

Effective January 11, 2004, the Office of Financial Services, OSS, centralized FDA relocation services with Prudential Relocation Services.

Services provided include: entitlement counseling, transportation of household goods, and travel voucher review and preparation. Access http://eric.fda.gov to view the on-line "Agency-wide Relocation Policy Guide" which provides basic administrative information for employees transferring from one duty station to another within the FDA.

Advance of Funds

You will use your government-issued credit card to obtain a cash advance from an ATM machine, for official government business only. Ensure your Travel Authorization contains a statement authorizing you to obtain cash advances and the amount authorized. ATM cash advances may be used to purchase samples. There are usually two fees associated with an ATM cash advance.

The "Terminal Fee" assessed by the ATM terminal's owner/supplier and the "Cash Advance Fee" assessed by the bank. Currently, the Cash Advance Fee is 1.5% of the total ATM advance; or 1.5% x $(Cash advance amount + ATM Terminal Fee). The Cash Advance Fee is described in your credit card agreement. These amounts must be included on the Travel Authorization/Voucher along with receipts before reimbursement can be made.

If you do not have a government travel card and are required to travel, please see your administrative officer about receiving a travel advance. For further information, see Staff Manual Guide 2343.1 Government Travel Card and ATM Advance Programs.

Claims for Reimbursement

Within five days after each trip, submit your electronic claim for reimbursement (Travel Voucher) using GovTrip. Expenses for local travel for meetings and/or field work are also claimed using GovTrip. All travel vouchers are processed electronically. See www.govtrip.com for web-based training information.

Travel Voucher Preparation-Clerical procedures vary from district to district, so consult your supervisor or administrative officer for instructions. State all items in chronological order. Show your mode of transportation and if accompanied, the names of the other travelers.

Show your date of departure and return to your official duty station, and when periods of leave commence and end. Show all points where costs are incurred.

Mandatory Statements Required on GovTrip-See IOM Exhibit 1-1 for allowable expenses, receipts required, etc.

Leave Taken in Travel Status-If you take any type of leave while in travel status, include a statement on your travel voucher that you apprised your timekeeper of the amount and type of leave taken. The timekeeper must initial your voucher to show that the leave has been recorded.

Reimbursable Expenses-Explain the necessity for unusual expenditures such as rental equipment, stenographic services and emergency charges. The following cash purchases are reimbursable when accompanied by necessary receipts (see Documentation below):

1. Travel costs such as road and bridge tolls, storage and parking for government cars, and handling of official (not personal) baggage.
2. Costs for samples and the necessary casual labour charges for their collection and packing. (See IOM 4.1.4.1(4) Official Samples.)
3. Telephone and telegraph expenses. Document that the use was for official purposes. For local telephone calls, show the number of calls only and the total cost each day.
4. Emergency purchases (flashlights, batteries, photographic film, jars, or dry ice for samples, etc.)
5. Coveralls or lab coat laundry while in travel status
6. Personal laundry while in travel status within continental U.S. (CONUS) for four or more consecutive nights

Documentation-Except for samples, all cash payments should be supported by itemized invoices or receipts signed by vendor, if possible. If you are unable to furnish receipts when submitting your voucher, explain that on the voucher.

Receipts for registration fees at meetings are required regardless of the amount. See Exhibit 1-1.

Telephone Communications

Commercial-Local, official telephone calls are reimbursable. When placing an official call from a non-government phone, use your government-issued calling card, call collect if permitted by your District"s policy, or call commercially and claim reimbursement on your travel voucher.

Commercial calls from hotels or motels should be made using your government-issued calling card, whenever possible. If not possible, they should be claimed on your travel voucher and be supported by the phone bill.

Calls made using a personal credit card or similar billing arrangements should be claimed on your travel voucher if a receipt is available at the time of voucher preparation. Otherwise, a follow-up petty cash voucher should be submitted, supported by a copy of your itemized phone bill, and certification the charge was for official government business.

Calls To Residence-FDA has established the following guidelines under which an employee in travel status for more than one night within the U.S. may be reimbursed for telephone calls home:

1. Calls should be made as economically as possible.
2. Calls should be made on the FTS network when possible. If not possible, calls should be made using your government-issued calling card. Telephone calls made with government-issued calling cards are automatically billed to the FDA. You are reimbursed through the voucher system when a surcharge is imposed for credit card calls from the traveler"s motel/ hotel room. Refer to Staff Manual Guide 2343.2 to determine the maximum allowable reimbursement for telephone calls home.

Districts that have differing union-negotiated agreements regarding telephone calls home while in travel status should be guided by those agreements.

Itineraries

Since situations arise which necessitate contacting you while in travel status, provide your supervisor with a travel itinerary listing where and how you can be reached.

Leave

Annual, compensatory, and sick leave is charged in one-quarter hour increments. Prior approval must be obtained from your supervisor for all leave, whenever possible. If this is not possible, advise your supervisor within the first hour of your workday when you will not be on duty.

Questions relating to leave should be directed to your immediate supervisor. If it is necessary for you to take leave while in travel status, notify your supervisor immediately. Include a specific statement on your travel voucher that you did so.

Refer to the NTEU Collective Bargaining Agreement dated 10/1/99 or the agreement negotiated at your local site for additional information regarding leave issues.

Disclosure of Official Information

You are not to release or divulge any information obtained during FDA investigative or inspectional operations, unless you are authorized to do so and the sharing (regardless of the manner) complies with FDA's information disclosure laws and procedures.

This includes information contained in diaries and field notes, except for official issuance of forms or documents to addressees. Do not release any originals or copies of reports, memos, diaries, forms (e.g.: FDA-483, 484, 464, etc.), or similar investigational documents to anyone outside the Agency without express concurrence of district or regional management and without following FDA''s laws and procedures (21 CFR 20.85-federal, 21 CFR 20.88-state/local, 21 CFR 20.89-foreign, 21 CFR Part 20-Freedom of Information Act (FOIA), and 21 CFR Part 21-Privacy Act).

Subpoena

If you are served a subpoena (commanding your appearance in court) or a subpoena duces tecum, (commanding the production of any record or testimony, or the giving of information relating to official FDA matters), immediately advise your supervisor.

You will be instructed by your District officials as to the proper procedures and actions on your part in complying with the subpoena. See 21 CFR 20.1, 20.2 and the Regulatory Procedures Manual (RPM) chapter 10-8, "Testimony; Production of Records; Certification of Records."

Requests by the Public, Including Trade

Be guided by IOM 1.4.4 on requests for information desired by the public under the Freedom of Information Act (FOIA). Refer to FDA's "Information Disclosure Manual" (IDM) for procedures for sharing non-public information with federal, state, local, or foreign government officials. (See IOM 1.4.3).

In the case of complaints where a sample has been collected from the complainant, your District may inform the complainant of FDA's findings when an examination is actually made of the sample. When you collect a sample from a complainant, and he asks for analytical results, he may be told that the FDA will advise him by letter of the general nature of the findings. See IOM 4.1.7 and IOM 4.4.6.3 for cautions on collecting this type sample.

Sharing Non-public Information with other Government Officials

If you receive requests for non-public information from officials of other federal agencies or from state, local or foreign government officials, be guided by the current IDM published by the Division of Compliance Policy (DCP) (HFC-230). You may not share FDA non-public information with such officials without being authorized to do so under FDA's procedures.

The procedures contained in the IDM on disclosing information to the public or sharing non-public information with officials from other federal agencies, or from state, local, or foreign governments were formerly found in Chapter 8 of the FDA's RPM. With the publication of the IDM, this material no longer appears in the RPM.

The most current IDM is available on the FDA Intranet by visiting the Office of Enforcement's website. Relevant sections on non-public disclosure may be found in the IDM, Section 4 as follows:

1. Sharing Non-Public Information with Foreign Government Officials,
2. Sharing Non-Public Information with Federal Government Officials,
3. Sharing Non-Public Information with State and Local Government Officials

Freedom of Information Act

Public Law 89-487, the Public Information section of the Administrative Procedures Act, more commonly known as the FOIA, adopts a general rule that, except where specifically exempt, all documents in government files shall be made available to the public.

There are various exemptions in certain areas, and it is these that mostly affect your operations in FDA. The regulations exempt certain information, such as personal privacy, deliberative process, open investigatory, as well as a company's trade secrets or confidential commercial information.

Procedures

Study and become familiar with the general provisions of the FOIA and the regulations in the Code of Federal Regulations (CFR) regarding the release of information to the public. In particular, study 21 CFR Parts 20 and 21, and 21 CFR 71.15, 171.1, 314.430, 514.11, 514.12 and others, all of which contain provisions regarding confidentiality in various FDA records and documents. See also, the RPM, subchapter 8, "Freedom of Information Act" and the IDM.

In addition to the FOIA, various other Acts such as the Federal Food, Drug, and Cosmetic (FD&C) Act, the Public Health Services (PHS) Act, and 18 U.S.C. 1905 each contain information relating to the confidentiality of information in government files, and are of particular interest. Special care should be taken to protect the identity of confidential sources. See IOM 5.2.9 for further guidance.

Requests for Documents

No field FDA employee has authority to deny any request for documents, no matter what form the request takes. Authority to deny requests rests with the Associate Commissioner for Public Affairs. Each field and district office is responsible for the internal handling of requests. Information disclosure personnel, e.g. FOI Officers, designated by their respective RFDD"s, are responsible for coordinating the implementation of the regulations, for development of procedures within their organization to handle requests, and for adherence to FDA"s laws and procedures regarding the maintenance of confidentiality of non-public information.

If you receive a request for information under the FOIA, advise the requester to write to the Food and Drug Administration, Division of Freedom of Information (HFI-35), 5600 Fishers Lane, Rockville, MD 20857.

Safety

Safety is a responsibility of FDA employees, their supervisors, and the Agency's management. These responsibilities include:

1. The reporting of any hazards or suspected hazards
2. Taking the necessary safeguards to minimize the opportunity for safety problems.

The Agency cannot permit employees or supervisors to disregard established or otherwise reasonable safety precautions and thereby place themselves and/or their fellow employees and/or the Agency's facilities at risk.

Be alert for problems associated with defective or misused equipment or supplies and their possible impact on patients and/or users. Contact your supervisor and/or the headquarters contacts listed in the applicable compliance program as necessary for assessment.

The home district of the manufacturer should be notified of product misuse, so it may be brought to the manufacturer's attention for consideration of precautionary labelling or redesign of the product.

Fully document these problems, to include the hazard and/or defect observed and whether user actions could be a contributing factor. Documentation should present sufficient data, such as photos and diagrams, to supplement a narrative describing the situation as well as the collection of samples.

When conducting an inspection or collecting a sample in a facility which requires donning personal protective equipment, guidance should be provided by the firm's management as follows:

1. Information about the specific hazards that may be encountered
2. The potential concentrations of these hazards
3. The personnel protective equipment determined to protect against these hazards

The firm's management should be able to provide you with documentation showing how these hazards were determined, what the expected exposures are and how they relate to the Occupational Safety and Health Administration's (OSHA) Permissible Exposure Limit (PEL). It should also offer information about the personal protective equipment that will protect you against a hazardous exposure. If you have any doubts about the hazards or the equipment recommended or provided to protect against them, do not enter these areas. Your Regional Industrial Hygienist or the Office of Regulatory Affairs (ORA) Safety and Occupational Health Manager may be able to help you evaluate the information provided to you, or furnish information regarding the hazard and the recommended personal protective equipment.

If you do not have the specific personal protective equipment recommended by the firm's management, have your District furnish what you need. In some cases, the firm may be willing to provide the necessary personal protective equipment, however if respiratory protection is required, you should not wear any respiratory protection unless your District has a written Respiratory Protection Program and you have been certified by your District's Respiratory Protection Program Administrator as having currently met the requirements of this program. It is ultimately your responsibility to ensure that you do not expose yourself to any hazard.

BIBLIOGRAPHY

Adam, R.: *Elements of Government,* New York, Random House, 1960.

Alex S. Jones: *The Trust: The Private and Powerful Family Behind the New York Times,* New York, Little Brown and Company, 1999.

Austin, Granville: *The Indian Constitution: Cornerstone of a Nation*, Oxford, Clarendon Press, 1966.

Baker, C. Edwin: *Advertising and a Democratic Press,* Princeton NJ: Princeton University Press, 1994.

Ball, Rick: *Meet the Press: Fifty Years of History in the Making,* New York, McGraw-Hill, 1998.

Blanchard, Margaret A.: *History of the Mass Media in the United States, An Encyclopedia,* Chicago, Fitzroy Dearborn Publishers, 1998.

Blau, M.: *Bureaucracy in Modern Society,* New York, Random House, 1956.

Brennen, Bonnie and Hanno Hardt: *Picturing the Past: Media, History and Photography*, Champaign, IL: University of Illinois Press, 1999.

Cannadine, David: *History and the Media*, New York, Palgrave Macmillian, 2004.

Carey, James W.: *Public Opinion and the Communication of Consent,* New York: Guilford Publications, 1995.

Clint C. Wilson.: *A History of the Black Press,* Washington, DC: Howard University Press, 1997.

Cook, T.: *Making Laws & Making News*, Washington, DC: Brookings, 1989.

Dahlgren, Peter and Colin Sparks: *Communication and Citizenship: Journalism and the Public Sphere in the New Media Age,* New York: Routledge, 1991.

Daniel, Webster: *The Media in America,* Santa Barbara, ABC-CLIO, 1995.

Dardenne, Robert: *A Free and Responsible Student Press: An Ideal Vision of How Community and Communication Can Preserve Scholastic Journalism,* St.Petersburg, The Poynter Institute for Media Studies, 1996.

David, B.: *The Civil War and the Press,* New Brunswick, NJ: Transaction Publishers, 2000.

Dizard, Jr. Wilson: *Old Media/New Media: Mass Communi-cation in the Information Age,* New York, Longman, 2000.

Downing, John: *Ethnic Minority Media: An International Perspective,* Thousand Oaks, CA: Sage, 1992.

Dwight, L. Teeter, Jr.: *Voices of a Nation: A History of Mass Media in the United States,* Needham Heights, Allyn & Bacon, 1997.

Earl, R.: *Writing for Mass Communication,* White Plains, NY: Longman, 1996.

Edwin Emery, and Nancy L. Roberts: *The Press and America: An Interpretive History of the Mass Media,* Boston, Allyn and Bacon, 1999.

Emery, Michael, Edwin Emery, and Nancy L. Roberts: *The Press and America: An Interpretive History of the Mass Media,* Boston, Allyn and Bacon, 1999.

Fishkin, James S.: *Democracy & Deliberation,* New Haven CT: Yale University Press, 1991.

Folkerts, Jean, and Dwight L. Teeter, Jr.: *Voices of a Nation: A History of Mass Media in the United States,* Needham Heights, Allyn & Bacon, 1997.

Friedrich, J.: *Constitutional Government and Democracy,* Boston, Ginn, 1950.

Ganggopadhyay, D. K.: *Revenue Administration in Assam,* Assam, Revenue Department, Government of Assam, 1990.

George, H.: *Toward a New Public Administration: The Minnowbrook Perspective,* San Francisco, Chandler, 1971.

Gerald, J. : *Handbook of Research Methods in Public Administration,* New York, Marcel Dekker, 1999.

Ghiglione, Loren:*The American Journalist: Paradox of the Press,* Washington, Library of Congress, 1990.

Gillmor, Dan: *We the Media: Grassroots Journalism by the People, for the People,* Sebastopol, CA: O'Reilly Media, 2004.

Graber, Doris A.: *Processing the News,* N.Y., Longman, 1984.

Hanno, Hardt: *Picturing the Past: Media, History and Photography,* Champaign, IL: University of Illinois Press, 1999.

Hansen, Kathleen A. and Nora Paul: *Behind the Message: Information Strategies for Communicators,* Boston, Allyn & Bacon, 2004.

Henry, Lewis: *The Black Press in the Middle West, 1865-1985,* Westport, CT: Greenwood Press, 1996.

Hudson, Frederick: *Journalism in the United States from 1690-1872,* New York, Routledge, 2000.

Kaye, Barbara K. and Norman J. Medoff.: *The World Wide Web: A Mass Communication Perspective,* Mountain View, CA: Mayfield Publishing Company, 1999.

Kellner, Douglas: *Television and the Crisis of Democracy,* Boulder, CO. Westview Press, 1990.

Kessler, Lauren: *The Dissident Press,* Newbury Park, CA: Sage, 1984.

Kitano, Harry: *The Ethnic Press in the United States,* Westport, CT: Greenwood Press, 1987.

Kumar, D.: *Administration Report of the Political Agency,* Agartala, Tripura State Cultural Research Institute & Museum, 1995.

Langman, Larry: *The Media in the Movies*, Jefferson, NC: McFarland & Company, 1997.

Lapchick, Richard E.: *Mass Politics: The Politics of Popular Culture*, New York, NY: St. Martin's/WORTH, 1999.

Margaret, A.: *History of the Mass Media in the United States, An Encyclopedia*, Chicago, Fitzroy Dearborn Publishers, 1998.

Martin, Paul E.: *Black Press, Britons and Immigrants: Alternative Press and Society*, Kingston, Jamaica: Vintage Communications, 1998.

Nancy L. Roberts: *The Press and America: An Interpretive History of the Mass Media*, Boston, Allyn and Bacon, 1999.

Norris, Pippa: *Women, Media and Politics*, Oxford, Oxford University Press, 1997.

Peddleton, E.: *Public Administration and the Public Interest*, New York, McGraw-Hill, 1936.

Prahlad, K.: *Governance and Public Administration for Poverty Reduction*, Salvador, Brazil, 1997.

Robert, T.: *Practical Public Management*, New York, Marcel Dekker, 1995.

Robert, V.: *Mass Media*, New York, Garland Publishing, 1987.

Robert, W.: *Public Bureaucracy and the Incentive Problem*, Washington, D.C., World Bank, 1994.

Ross, Karen: *Making the Local News: Local Journalism in Context*, London, Routledge, 1998.

Simon, D. : *Public Administration*, New York, Knopf, 1950.

Sloan, W. David: *Perspectives on Mass Communication History*, Hillsdale, NJ: Lawrence Erlbaum, 1991.

Thomas, Leonard: *The Power of the Press: The Birth of American Political Reporting*,New York, Oxford University Press, 1986.

Wade, R.: *Public Bureaucracy and the Incentive Problem*, Washington, D.C., World Bank, 1994.

Index

A

B

C

D

E

□□□